PEOPLE WHO CARE

People Who Care

C. W. Brister

BROADMAN PRESS
Nashville, Tennessee

© Copyright 1967 BROADMAN PRESS
Nashville, Tennessee
All rights reserved

422-505

Second Printing

All Scripture quotations are taken from the
Revised Standard Version of the Bible unless otherwise indicated.

DEWEY DECIMAL CLASSIFICATION NUMBER: 262
Library of Congress Catalog Card Number: 67-17424
Printed in the United States of America

2.5N68KSP

to
James and Tunis Harris
John and Bettye McNaughton
Clarence and Renita Duncan

friends of God and men

Preface

People who care in the modern world are a rare breed. When a friend heard the title of this book, he replied dubiously: "You mean there are still some of *those* people around?"

Frankly, in our competitive, often brutal, culture some citizens are uncertain about their own survival. They find little time for coping with issues that baffle overburdened neighbors. There has been much renewal talk by theologians since World War II. It is not evident, however, that Christian people are eagerly waiting to assume their own responsibility as men and women in mission.

Anyone who explores the secular setting for ministry is forced to admit that the church can no longer engage in familiar ministries in traditional ways and be successful. Varieties of ministry are not likely to diminish but rather to increase in years to come. Calls for renewal and flexibility may threaten congregations conscientiously involved in programs which they have learned and to which they have felt called. Few churches are willing to pioneer relevant ministries at the risk of failure or denominational disapproval.

Some critics, in calling for Christian action, have concluded that present structures such as residential congregations and denominations have outlived their usefulness.
They have challenged people to see where God is at work
in the world and to join him there. Abandoning the
church in favor of civil rights marches or Peace Corps
programs may be modern but unwise. We could dissipate
whatever talents and energies we have by simply attack-
ing the present church structures. This, however, avoids
getting at the heart of the problem.

A more difficult, yet prophetic, task lies before us. New
models of ministry must be devised for pastors and laymen, both in Christian churches and in secular societies.
Some old patterns of ministry must be revitalized, yet
retained. And Christian leaders performing such tasks
must equip themselves to survive the stress and tension
inherent in any process of transition. This is no easy assignment.

This book is addressed primarily to Christian laymen
who, as the church, live in the world of today and who
seek guidance for the unknown era of tomorrow. You are
not without information. Modern laymen have produced
their own curbstone versions of theology. Some readers,
out of a personal struggle of soul, have examined religion
in depth. God is very alive to them.

Yet subtle dangers lurk in the process of forming religious persuasions on the run. Reading résumés, discussing
digests, and listening to "pop" lectures about a travel-light
secular theology can confuse as well as inform a person.
One can accumulate a mishmash of cluttered ecclesiastical

jargon for use with nonchurch friends. A person may thread clichés and vogue names into Sunday School lessons and church enlistment conversations, yet discover his spiritual illiteracy in some ordinary experience of need.

For example, what do you say to the secularist— perhaps your business associate or an acquaintance—who finds no evidence of God in the physical universe? Is there a common core of wisdom upon which one may draw in coping with a youth who is a misfit? a divorcee who is a constant source of family embarrassment? an extremist who labels all intellectuals as instruments of the devil? a neighbor whose husband has died in an automobile accident? a friend or family member who has disappointed you?

Laymen who believe that Christ's ministry is the responsibility of the whole church are asking: "How does a concerned Christian exercise his calling in the modern world?" This volume addresses that question. It is designed for pastors and people who desire not only to attend worship services on Sunday but also to *be* God's church in the lively relationships and decisions of every day. You will discover the book's internal principle—*the ethic of a servant church*—in all that follows.

Several friends have read the manuscript and offered suggestions which I have taken seriously. I am grateful particularly to the William Hendersons, Clarence Duncans, John McNaughtons, Gene Mastons, and to my colleague Milton Ferguson who, during a "brain-storming" session at a coffee break, first proposed the book's title. Numerous students offered ideas and case notes from research, and Nannie Don Beaty carefully typed the final version of the manuscript.

Gloria, my wife, offered helpful suggestions and insisted that laymen should be spared preacher-talk. I am grateful for her tolerance of my idiosyncrasies and her unfailing love.

C. W. BRISTER

Contents

1

God's Purpose for the Church

"We would like for you to attend a band concert at the historic Moravian church here in Winston-Salem," my host announced. "Later, we can share a unique bread and coffee fellowship which is a part of their tradition."

"Is it a type of Communion service?" I inquired. "Not exactly," he replied, "but it has been an established practice with this Protestant sect for centuries. The Bohemian Brethren, as the disciples of reformist Peter Chelcicky called themselves, organized in 1467 and were reconstituted as Moravians in 1722. They have stuck pretty much to themselves, clustering in small communities, since their ancestors immigrated from Europe."

"Wasn't John Wesley influenced profoundly by a group of Moravians at the time he came to Georgia as a missionary to the Indians?" asked his wife. "Yes, it's the same group. You'll see how little they've changed. The Moravians are hard-working, pietistic folk who've tried to preserve five hundred years of tradition. They have never really moved into the twentieth century."

Our host had described a dying congregation, unwilling to modify its ministry to meet the challenging needs of urban people. We attended the worship service out of curiosity and historic interest. I expected the sermon to be a postmortem examination of a curious congregational corpse. But it was not a funereal occasion.

There was a lively service of hymns. A recent theological school graduate, who obviously had spent time in study and prayerful reflection upon God's Word, was introduced as the guest preacher. The sermon, rather than an autopsy, was a clear call to congregational action. His idea was "The Moravian Church—Museum or Mission?" He exposed the error of devotion to a limited, cultic tradition. Without ridicule or satire he chided the congregation's prejudices, shortcomings, and preoccupation with the past. Then he called the worshipers to repentance and urged commitment to their Christian responsibilities in the modern world.

"But," you may protest, "that brash young seminarian should not have disturbed the church. He may have embarrassed them!" You are correct to this extent. Youthful churchmen often see what is wrong rather than what is right with the church.[1]

On the other hand, God continually removes "Do Not Disturb" signs from church doors and human hearts. He always grows restless with man's aimless religiosity, his inclination for feasts and festivals, his denial of true righteousness (see Isa. 61:8; Hosea 4:1-6, 6:4-6; Amos 5:21-24; Matt. 25:31-46; Luke 16:10; 1 Cor. 13:4).

That dynamic preacher did not fail. Sensitive to the incarnation's true intent—God touching and transforming life through his Son—he asked his hearers to put away their cherished relics and to engage actively in community life as Christian witnesses.

Success Is Not Enough

In past generations Moravians had founded schools, constructed church buildings, and supported missionaries. Now they were being asked: "What does it mean to be God's people today?" They were reminded that fondness for the methods of past spiritual success was not enough. Christians must identify the work that a church should do now in its community.

This incident suggests a profound truth. *Christian faith seeks contemporary expression or else it withers in personal and social life.* Churches must be relevant and effective or perish. The nature and purpose of a church or group of churches requires action—ministry "in Christ's stead." This means more than institutional success. In addition to growing in membership and wealth, what are churches for? May a religious group be active, yet fail in the biblical sense to be the people of God? Consider the following facts.

Current surveys reveal that more than 98 percent of all United States citizens believe in God. This is true despite much publicity given the far-out "death of God" movement of the 1960's. Two out of three Americans belong to some religious group—Christian, Jewish, or a cult. Value of church properties—worship houses, schools, hospitals, and so on—exceeds three billion dollars. Electronic media like radio, television, and films permit religious groups to address vast audiences of listeners.

"What about *our* churches?" you ask. Southern Baptists hope to achieve a total membership of twelve million by 1970. We outnumber any other non-Catholic denomination in America. Annual cash receipts for the work of the churches approach 750 million dollars. Missionary efforts are far flung, reaching into more than sixty nations and spreading rapidly in all fifty states of the Union. The organizations are large. Sunday Schools, laymen's groups, women's work, and youth organizations are without parallel among Protestants in this country.

Churches continue to grow in numbers, programs, and administrative efficiency. Have God's people kept pace in understanding (1) what the gospel is and demands, (2) where Christian love leads a person, and (3) what a Christian should be? Because many members fail to practice their faith in life (James 4:17), some observers think that American churches are in trouble. According to one survey, nearly half of all persons interviewed felt that religion is losing its influence in personal and social affairs.[2] Also, the number of candidates for the ministry is lagging behind population growth.

Thinking Christians wonder at certain contradictions between (1) statistical success and moral failure, (2) the ideal of loving service and advancing church organizations, (3) Christendom's efforts at unity and competitive lack of unity, (4) cherished friends in redeemed fellowships and bitter congregational strife, (5) freedom in Christ and encroachment upon human liberty by both church and state. Is institutional success God's purpose for the church? If so, people should be taught to *produce* rather than to *care* by managers, not ministers, of the gospel. Are we safe in assuming that success, rightly interpreted, is the by-product (not the chief ambition) of a ministering church?

Christians—Cool or Committed Men?

Why do Christian people—Moravians or ourselves—need to be reminded of God's redemptive mission? One, because faith can become a pious habit—unused except on special occasions. Rather than a lively commitment to divine service, faith may be interpreted as fidelity to a theological position, devotion to a sectarian program, or participation in a clannish congregation. People thus preoccupied can lose their evangelical warmth and missionary intensity.

Again, church organizations, methods, and customs may become ends within themselves. "But," you protest, "aren't policies and programs essential?" They are essential for modern religious expression, but they must remain subject to the mind of Christ and the purpose of his gospel.

Christians, too, are tempted to live by a double standard of morality—private and public. Confusion of loyalties can pervert the ideal of being "in the world yet not of it," which is supposed to be distinctive of the church.

Part of the layman's confusion about the church, manifested as indifference or criticism, is an outgrowth of the Christian community's ambivalence about its mode of witness. Influenced by a theology of social change, some clergymen have abandoned traditional ministries in favor of the Peace Corps, politics, and protest movements like civil rights. The church is "now so isolated from the world . . . as to be irrelevant to its needs and forms, now so accommodated to that world as to be only the reflection and defender of the socially accepted values, now simply troubled and uncertain." [3] In light of such problems, what is happening to the man in the pew?

Because they detect contradictions and imperfections in churches, some sensitive Christians prefer to remain uninvolved. One layman confessed:

We have given up meaningful interest in the organized church at this stage. The local church as we've encountered it since 1956 is next to nothing as far as what we can give or need is concerned.

Personally, we don't feel that God is dead, but that some believers need a type of Christian fellowship which is pretty rarely found in organizations which must appeal to millions.

Some church members are mystified by the absence of the mind of Christ in their particular congregation. A devoted deacon, whose wife died unexpectedly, acknowledged that the four-thousand-member church to which he belonged failed him during that grief experience. "I walked the streets of our city at night," he confessed, "so lonely that I was tempted to seek fellowship with individuals in the bars and cheap hotels. No one knows what a wilderness experience that was!" Fortunately, he did not drift away from God.

An Episcopalian with whom I talked, a dentist in a city numbering over a million inhabitants, had "tried out" five different churches. The large downtown church left him cold. His wife and daughters were aggressive, mingled with the members, but he felt left out. Each suburban congregation they visited seemed to be a closed circle of people, intent on congratulating one another and content with themselves. In a time of anguished confusion he sought enhancement of life from several churches and failed to find it.

Other church attendants are indifferent. They attend worship when it is convenient but prefer to remain unencumbered with local church ties, financial support, and witnessing tasks. For example, approximately one fourth of all Southern Baptists do not hold membership in the place where they reside. The meaning and value of church membership do not seem clear to them. Such people have been lulled into indifference by formal connections with churches. Proclamation for them has become the repetition of holy words with a hollow ring.

Did this not happen in some Russian Orthodox churches prior to the revolution of 1918, and to the state churches in Germany as Dietrich Bonhoeffer knew them? [4]

The church has made an impact upon many individuals, however, who are engaged in useful living. A patient in a major medical center, awaiting heart surgery, was visited before the operation by his world-famous surgeon. Imagine his surprise when the medical specialist closed their visit with these words: "You had better talk with the Lord tonight, and I will too." A scientist wearing a physician's frock became temporarily a *pastor* to his patient on the eve of surgery. Such unpretentious Christian ministries could be multiplied in our overwhelming world.

A Changing World

The urgency of clarifying the church's nature and ministry has become clear as familiar landmarks disappear in a period of chaotic social change. Peter F. Drucker, management consultant and educator, has noted that "anyone over forty lives in a different world from that in which he came to manhood, lives as if he had emigrated, fully grown, to a new and strange country." [5] This observation is true whether one lives in Bangkok or Benton Harbor, Lisbon or Los Angeles, Cairo or Chicago, Hong Kong or Houston.

No sensitive person would deny the secularity and complexity of modern life. Years ago a farmer might hear a sermon at a July revival meeting and reflect on it for weeks as he plowed the fields, mended the harness, milked the cows, and gathered his crops. His life situation encouraged reliance upon the daily care of God. Today, we live in what Harvey Cox has called "the secular city." Secularism (from the Latin *saecularis*—worldly, pagan) implies a philosophy of life and conduct determined with reference to the present age. Thus modern man finds little in the world which reminds him of his Creator. His daily decisions are made frequently without reference to a personal God.

It is not easy for persons—distracted with many voices—to give undivided attention to the Word of God. Urbanism has become America's way of life. The surroundings in which metropolitan man's life is spent are vastly more complex than the simple rural culture of the nineteenth century. The family has disintegrated into individuals each of whom lives for himself and pursues his own goals in a mechanistic society. The patriarchal family (where father is head of the home) has given way to a permissive, democratic kind of authority.

Neighborhoods as a form of community and mutual care have become meaningless. There may be one commuter station, a local post office, schools, shops, and churches, but not one common purpose and uniting foundation. Catholics and Jews, once restricted to narrow sectors of cities because of foreign language barriers and prejudice, have broken out of their man-made ghettoes. Demolition crews, employed in urban renewal projects, assist in splitting up neighborhoods by destroying apartment dwellings, stores, and familiar landmarks.

Approximately one fifth of United States households move each year, hoping to improve economic and social status. This means that over eleven million families, or thirty-six million people move annually. The spiritual and psychological rootlessness that follows the loss of familiar ties and surroundings is destructive.

National population figures point beyond two hundred million American citizens. Civil rights legislation has freed—at least legally—about twenty million members of racially segregated groups for equal opportunities of education, employment, housing, and social status. While the percentage of citizens above sixty-five years of age remains fairly constant, the Census Bureau predicts that, by

1970, more than half of all Americans alive will be under twenty-five.

If this appraisal of social change is correct, churches must search for and find Christian relevance in a new, as yet nameless, era. Christian mission, and accordingly theology and education, must unfold in a context of secularization and uncontrollable change. What is clear in any case is this: We are in the presence of new possibilities, and new dangers, which point the way beyond the present limits of traditional ministry.

The Church's Task

Such circumstances force us to face the possibility that churches can lose their identity. Denominations can substitute institutional activities for soul-saving tasks. Laymen may look upon church membership as a sanctuary from life's storms or a hospital for sinners. In Arthur Miller's play *The Death of a Salesman,*[6] Willy Lohman, the leading character, loses interest in selling shoes. He seeks to escape boredom and failure through sexual exploits and visions of grandeur. At Willy's graveside funeral service, following his death as a suicide, his son Biff laments: "He didn't know who he was." Can Christians, too, lose the meaning of life which is found in obedience to God, comradeship with one another, and service to the world?

We have seen how the church's social context changes in varied cultures and periods of history. Its saving purpose, however, should not change! This suggests an important principle: *We must discover God's purpose for the church in each new generation.* Each congregation and denomination should inquire of the Lord what his will and purpose are for this new situation. It is from him that we gain wisdom and courage to live.

Writers of the New Testament—apostles, pastors, and teachers of the first century—did not think in *our* terms about the church. Little detailed, explicit information about the church's nature, life, and work can be determined authoritatively from the Scriptures.

Interestingly, only one of the four Gospel writers recalled that Jesus used the term "church," and he recorded its use on only two occasions. In Matthew 16:18, the concept is wholly spiritual and its origin attributed to Christ's initiative and man's response. The second instance, Matthew 18:17, refers to church discipline and implies, without any explanation, a brotherhood having social and organizational aspects. While our Lord perceived the church in a specific, local sense, there was implied a universal quality as well. The other Gospels assume the spiritual reality that constitutes the church without using the term "church" or defining any equivalent term.[7] We cannot conclude, as did Emil Brunner in *The Misunderstanding of the Church* (Philadelphia: Westminster Press, 1953), that the church as a communion of redeemed persons has nothing of the character of an institution about it.

1. *Jesus Christ created the church initially by calling individual persons to faith in himself.* When the Pharisees criticized him for talking with sinners, Jesus explained his purpose: "I came that they may have life, and have it abundantly" (John 10:10). The Bible takes for granted

that life, physical and spiritual, originates with God and that his Son makes this life externally visible (Gen. 1:27-31; John 1:1-13).

The New Testament term *ekklēsia,* translated "church," implies God's true congregation—persons called from sin and darkness into salvation and light. Those who believed the Word whom God sent, Jesus of Nazareth, became his followers—soldiers under his command. This is why the Jews accused him of sedition against Rome. Whereas the Roman soldier swore allegiance to his emperor, Jesus' disciples took an oath of loyalty to him alone (Acts 5:29).

Various terms are used in the Scriptures to describe the church's nature. Their rich symbolism and implications can help us identify the work that a church should do. Early Christians were so nicknamed, as followers of *the One,* by outsiders or pagans. He was their *Kyrios,* or commander, their leader, model, and Lord—as well as Saviour. They were not Caesar's but Christ's: the people of *God,* a colony of *heaven,* the temple of the *Holy Spirit,* a *royal* priesthood, a *holy* nation, *God's* building, the body of *Christ.*

Paradoxically, the church is *both* the universal (mystical) body of Christ *and* local congregations of believers.

2. *The church's first task is faithfulness to Christ her Lord.* There is only *one* ministry, and we are permitted to participate in it as God's partners. The apostle Paul said that this ministry belongs to Jesus, first, then to his church. "God was in Christ reconciling the world to himself . . . and entrusting to us the message of reconciliation. So we are ambassadors for Christ, God making his appeal

through us" (2 Cor. 5:19-20). Christians are ministers of the gospel of redemption.

This ministry is not something which belongs to one group (the ordained) within the church. God allows all his people to share in it. We are "workers together" with him to bring salvation to the world. Also, Christians should demonstrate a way of life which is valid for persons and nations. In chapter 2, I shall make explicit the layman's part in this partnership.

3. *We may identify the church's ministry, and our own, by recalling key incidents in Jesus' ministry.* First, what was the passion that prompted Jesus to leave his Heavenly Father's house and to identify with citizens of earth? He refused the fame and fortune of an earthly empire (Luke 4:1-13). Human praise and approval, or criticism and hostility, did not throw him off course. In Matthew 23:37, he is seen weeping over the spiritual burdens and physical needs of ancient Jerusalem's multitudes. Fortunately our Lord did more than cry. He identified with men held in the grip of moral chaos and a religion of fear. "He had compassion for them, because they were harassed and helpless, like sheep without a shepherd" (Matt. 9:36). Love carried him to Calvary that he might give eternal life to all who would believe in his name (John 3:16).

Second, we find Jesus' concept of his ministry, and therefore of ours, expressed on a return visit to his hometown synagogue (read Luke 4:16 f.).

And he came to Nazareth, where he had been brought up; and he went to the synagogue, as his custom was, on the sabbath day. And he stood up to read; and there was given to him the book of the prophet Isaiah. He opened the book and found the place where it was written, "The Spirit of the Lord is upon me, because he has anointed me [here is the ministry] to preach good news to the poor. He has sent me to proclaim release to the captives and recovering of sight to the blind, to set at liberty those who are oppressed, to proclaim the acceptable year of the Lord." And he closed the book, and gave it back to the attendant, and sat down; and the eyes of all in the synagogue were fixed on him. And he began to say to them, "Today this scripture has been fulfilled in your hearing."

His words, based upon Isaiah 61:1-2, found acceptance and approval among the hearers. They spoke well of him as "Joseph's son," a hometown boy who had made good.

The climate of their conversation changed considerably, however, when Jesus recalled Old Testament instances when God's gracious action included non-Jews: (1) Elijah sent to the widow of Zarephath in the land of Sidon, and (2) Elisha's cleansing a Syrian leper, Naaman, a nonbeliever. "When they heard this, all in the synagogue were filled with wrath. And they rose up and put him out of the city, and led him to the brow of the hill on which their city was built, that they might throw him down headlong. But passing through the midst of them he went away" (Luke 4:28-30).

"Why were they prompted to chase Jesus out of town and to pitch him off a cliff?" you ask. Jesus annoyed the Jewish covenant community because he insisted that God's love is universal. It includes the sinners, poor, handicapped, captives, and oppressed persons everywhere.

Furthermore, he failed to work through approved channels of the Jewish hierarchy with the chief priests and elders. Refusing to discriminate or conform to their prejudices, Jesus called all kinds of people to do his work.

The Messiah of God proclaimed a new covenant of salvation that was sealed in his suffering love upon the cross. We learn from him that service to persons must cross all human barriers of race, culture, politics, and social standing. The gospel is at home in every situation of human need. Churches today must find ways to remove or transcend barriers that separate their members from other persons and groups. Christ's lordship must be extended to *all the world* where personality is blighted by sin, social disadvantages, physical handicaps, and mental disorders. This requires skill and mutually planned action.

4. *The church's tasks are basic, continuing activities, undertaken in obedience to Christ's command and example.* The church may be viewed as a fellowship of ultimate concerns. It is not some celestial body of invisible saints. Rather, it is a spiritual brotherhood of persons who are committed to Christ and the advancement of his kingdom. Thus the Christian's ultimate loyalty is to Christ, the one true head of the church.

The basic biblical word for the local fellowship of Christ's followers is *koinōnia,* implying a ministering congregation. *They are people who care.* By its very nature the Christian *koinōnia* involves a shared ministry by all the *laos*—the people of God. This includes pastors and people alike. Thus the church is an organism, Christ's body, requiring identification through baptism and obedience in discipleship. It is under orders to change the world (Matt. 28:19-20). In every age and culture this vital organism, Christ's body, expresses its life through organized forms or churches.

What is the church for? Primarily, the congregation lives for God's sake in worship, for the world's sake in proclamation and witness, and for its own sake in nurture and ministry. It lives out the kingdom of God in specific communities across the world in every period of history. The church's mission of witnessing and ministry forms the basis of discussion in the remaining chapters of this book.

At the outset we should affirm that Christian living "worthy of the gospel" requires the presence and guidance of the Holy Spirit. The *new* humanity about which the apostles wrote is the fellowship of God's Spirit (1 Cor. 3:17). We rely upon his power to interpret the mind of Christ, to convict consciences and cleanse from sin, and to guide members of congregations in ways of righteousness. God's Spirit makes the church's task possible and worthwhile (John 14:16-17; Acts 1:4-5,8).

Today's layman also believes that God is active in his rapidly changing world. He seeks to discover where God is working and to join him there. This raises a new question. What does it mean to be a responsible layman in the twentieth century?

2

The Emergent New Layman

I wish to be identified with those persons who are convinced that the church's mission is shared by all Christians—the *laos*—who are God's people.[1] This includes the laity—all men, women, and young people in a general ministry—as well as the clergy—God's set-apart, ordained representatives. A layman is anyone who seeks to live in obedience to Christ, both in and beyond his church. He is a Christian who declines the role of a professional religionist. He prefers to remain an amateur; not a dabbler, but a lover seeking competence in the Christian way of life.

In the remainder of this chapter I shall use the terms "laity" or "layman" for all servants of the gospel, and the term "minister" for the set-apart, duly ordained clergyman. This is done solely for clarity, for I believe that God uses all his people as servants of the gospel wherever they work in the world.

A part of our consideration will be to distinguish the role of the Christian pastor from that of the layman in this interrelated ministry.

A Portrait of the Layman

In attempting to trace the new layman's profile we must first sketch a composite portrait, based upon models in varied situations. This layman is not one man but every man in Christ's kingdom. Sometimes he is venturesome, more often cautious. Perhaps he is concerned about the wrong things, such as striving for status in relationships; and he is always subject to the fear of dying.

Laymen include white middle-class Protestants *and* people of color, the educated elite *and* socially disadvantaged minority, disciplined executives *and* disorderly teen-agers, spiritually sound *and* morally baffled young adults, persons searching for self-discovery *and* others who are merely trying to survive in our chaotic society.

"Yes, but . . . what is *new* about him?" you ask. "Isn't the layman like the poor—with us always?" Early Christianity failed to distinguish between those gifted persons whom God assigned to formal church offices and all the other members who were God's servants, too. The term "pastor" in the New Testament originally implied a *function* performed and later was applied to an *office* held in church life. Pastoral (or caring) functions—reconciling, healing, supporting, and teaching—were performed by many unofficial ministers (1 Cor. 12:12-28; Eph. 4:7-12; Rom. 12:5-8). Each member used his God-given talents (gifts of the Spirit) where there was need. Jesus, in the story of the good Samaritan, taught the wisdom of being close at hand in ministry (Luke 10:25-37). Helpfulness among God's people is often determined by where, not who, one is.

As churches developed, elders or bishops were appointed by the apostles to exercise pastoral guidance over congregations. Deacons (from *diakonoi,* meaning "servants") were ordained as their associates in such tasks as direction, preaching, pastoral care, and worship leadership. In time, while not implied in the Scriptures, the services of clergy and laity separated into two distinct spheres and callings.

A justifiable interpretation of the common man's occupation as "vocation" or "calling" was not achieved in the Middle Ages. Nor were the Protestant reformers agreed upon the layman's role. Luther gave high religious significance to the layman's calling, but he interpreted it mainly in terms of passive resignation to the will of God. One was to serve God in his place and social station in life as best he or she could and stay there. Luther identified readily with Germany's princes but not with her poor.

John Calvin's church in Geneva had no place for the economic parasite, rich or poor. He upheld a man's vocation as the "chief part of human life," that which is of most importance before God. Unlike Luther, he taught that a man might change his vocation if it served the glory of God. Calvin advocated vocational activism, under religious sanction, which has had revolutionary results in modern economic and social life. Accordingly, he has come to be regarded as the chief prophet of capitalism and the industrial revolution.

At this point we should note the difference between the minister and the layman. The Christian minister feels called by God to understand and proclaim the gospel, to lead people in worship and work, and to guide them in the disciplines of Christian living. This divine commission is to devote his whole being, as a living sacrifice, to the church's redemptive mission. He is no dearer to the heart of God than is any devoted layman, yet there is no turning back from a full lifetime of service. Whatever difference there may be between them resides primarily in degree and quantity rather than in direction and quality of ministry.

Today, we recognize that the minister's role is to "equip the saints" for their own task of ministering—in family life, in daily work, in the church, and in the world. Terms like "catalyst," "coach," "enabler," and "quarterback" have been proposed in lieu of the traditional "minister of the Word" to describe the pastor's teaching task. We don't need to argue about such phrases, but we should magnify the layman's need for a model in an era of complacency.

Yet ministers do not have to remake church members in their own image. They should exhibit evidence of walking with Christ and claim opportunities for helping people, knowing that laymen will follow a respected example. Kenneth Chafin warns laymen not to become "little preachers," aping some prominent clergyman and testifying subjectively to one experience as if it were standard or typical.[2] God should be permitted to use each Christian's life, interests, and aptitudes as he wills.

Change Can Be Confusing

Laymen confess that the tremendous changes occurring in economics, politics, international affairs, family life, and morality create insecurity and soul-searching for them. Some of them, mistakenly, are attempting to isolate Sunday's religious experiences from weekday decisions and commitments. Such a division between sacred and secular things is the seedbed for self-deception, neuroses, and a functional atheism in life. God's concern is with the whole man—material and spiritual—not merely with some spirit-like part of him.

In this atomic age one year sees more changes than an entire decade before the forties. Change does not necessarily mean deterioration. It may mean growth. But change involves looking at things that disturb us and charting a course of action toward goals that are Christian.

What bothers the layman?

1. *Many Christians detect little difference between the values of the secular, business world and the values of the churches.* When an imported crystal chandelier crashed from the ceiling of a church auditorium under construction some members wondered if the Lord was displeased with their new, palatial building. The getting and possessing of things presently dominates society. Like their parents, adolescents want automobiles primarily as status symbols rather than for transportation. An administrator of a high school, with a student body of over three thousand, confessed that 80 percent of the boys drove their own cars. "It's our biggest headache," he added. And it is for parents, too.

By their increased assets, comfortable buildings, and mushrooming budgets churches almost seem to be encouraging materialism among members. Critics call the church's attempt to harmonize Christian and social values "culture religion." [3] Service may be equated with worship attendance and financial support. Furthermore, worship may *not* lead to renewal. For example, salesmen at church, intent upon closing a deal on Monday, may be unaware of God and insensitive to the actual needs of their customers as persons. Teen-agers who sing in the Chapel choir on Sunday morning may park and pet on some lovers' lane that night.

2 *Modern man is uncertain how he should think about God.* Just as some collegians and laymen were making a little sense of what contemporary theologians were saying, theology in the 1960's appeared to go into a tailspin.

"What is theology?" you may ask, "and what is its task?" Theology is man's reflected response to God's revelation in deed and in word. It is man's appraisal of God and of his own life in the world before God. In a sense, each believer must work out his own notions about God and the Christian life. Each congregation and denomination must compose its own theology according to historic understandings of the faith and its unique social context.

Laymen are baffled by "death of God" talk, and rightly so. Thomas J. J. Altizer [4] spoke recently at a nearby university. During his televised appearance Altizer admitted that, for him, God was literally dead and had disappeared from history. Since it was a morning lecture, most of his TV viewers were women who were confused by his comments.

A lady called me that evening. "Is God really dead," she exploded, "or is that guy Altizer some kind of nut? I need help. Jack and I have a hard enough time trying to live up to our faith as it is. If God is gone, we may as well quit the church!"

The limited space and larger concerns of this book do not permit a full discussion of the doctrine of God. Briefly, however, how would you have responded to a confused friend who has never enjoyed much security in this world? Telling her that families who "pray together stay together" would have mocked her concern.

I listened to her negative feelings, then reminded her that, long ago, God himself beckoned man to belief. When the prophet Jeremiah sought evidence of God during a period of discouragement, the Lord said: "Call to me and I will answer you, and will tell you great and hidden things which you have not known" (Jer. 33:3). The psalmist acknowledged that "deep calls to deep" (Psalm 42:7). God's magnetism for man draws him from sin and selfishness into a trusting relationship of spiritual wholeness.

3. *The new layman feels inadequate against rivals of the Christian faith—varieties of unbelief.* Let's admit it. We are frightened! Twentieth-century humpty-dumpty life has fallen off history's wall. Responsible men ask: "Can life be put together again?"

Christians are experiencing a failure of moral courage. An executive confessed that in seeking to abide by New Testament principles he had cost his company a half million dollars in one business deal. With right and wrong in sexual relations being blurred by the "Playboy philosophy," young people are left to flounder in uncertainty.

God's people are experiencing a breakdown of values. It is possible to be between twenty-five and thirty years of age and never to have known a world without war. Children in many lands cut their teeth in a war climate of hate and mistrust. The atheistic philosophy of communism now controls one third of the earth's population. American servicemen battle enemies on varied fronts, while citizens at home face internal invaders: family disruption, delinquency, the "sexplosion," and racial strife.

"You Can't Go Home Again"

Like ancient Israel on the wilderness road from Egypt to Canaan, there is no turning back for the new layman. His footsteps move relentlessly toward some unknown promised land. He may disagree with Bonhoeffer, who said that man has "come of age" and is done with God in the traditional sense.[5] But he knows that there is a new outlook abroad in the world—an outlook independent, international, and alive.

Some ostrich-like people with whom I talk hope to turn back the calendar by wishful thinking. "What has changed?" they ask, pretending to be "jes' plain folks" who believe what they have always believed. Remove the mask, however, and their hurts, fears, pride in their children, and confidence in new resources slip into view. Like Professor Higgins in *My Fair Lady*, who claimed to be "just an ordinary man," they may not be good examples of the simplicity they profess.

A visitor in such a home may see a soldier son's picture, of World War II vintage, displayed on a table or mantle.

The question "Is this your son?" stirs repressed memories of aging parents. They tell how an uncomplicated boy—fresh, clean, suitcase in hand—left the farm in the 1940's, never to return. Or, if he survived his education to hate and kill the enemy, the confusion of military existence, the temptations of men in uniform, and, perhaps, an internment camp experience, he was probably never the same. Oriented to new patterns of life, in Thomas Wolfe's words, he was unable to come home again.

Obtaining a postwar education at government expense, the GI Joe of twenty-five years ago has become an urbanite. Though fifty-four million people still live in rural areas, only about 7 percent of the United States population are farmers. Whether in the city or country *the new layman's mode of life and thought is shaped by city life.*

He prefers bakery bread and pasteurized milk, a modern house with all the conveniences, educational advantages for his children, one or two late-model cars, favorite TV programs, excellent medical care, an up-to-date insurance program, and a cemetery plot that assures perpetual care. He has much more than his parents possessed on the farm. Yet their steady aim, tranquility of spirit, and enjoyment of God's creation seem to elude his grasp.

Now in his middle years, the veteran of World War II wants to do something worthwhile. After relating how his life had been spared during enemy action, a neighbor said wistfully: "God must have saved me for a purpose."

Today's layman hopes to follow through on his wish to make a better world. Can he do it? This goal seems to be in the realm of the spirit and requires religious resources for attainment. Certainly, without a radical Christian devotion man will perish in his broken world.

I want to be hopeful, but something tempers my enthusiasm. In our highly specialized, technical society there are more and more people who do not know what they are doing. Other men or machines do much of their thinking for them. All of the evidence calls for a new breed of Christian laymen who (1) possess insight into what is really happening in the world, and who (2) will prepare themselves to change the world today and tomorrow.

Breaking the Organizational Barrier

Could it be that going to church is not sufficient for Christian mission? Perhaps. Yet, as one celebrates his faith in God through worship, he is witnessing to his neighbors. Some men think that they must leave the church in order to engage the world redemptively. Others call for putting an end to the institutional church and expressing faith through Christian action.[6] Yet the Bible asserts that "Christ loved the church and gave himself up for her" (Eph. 5:25). He expects his followers to *be* the church in the world.

How, then, may someone who wishes to live "where the action is" move beyond organizational ties alone and bring the gospel to life in his corner of the world? Lawyer William Stringfellow suggests that "Christians must enter the common life of the world fully and unequivocally in order to know the Word of God, in order to witness to the Word of God in the world, in order to worship God at all."[7] He has practiced this advice by providing legal services to members of economically deprived minority groups at minimum costs. This Episcopal layman is saying that divine worship in solemn assemblies and devoted work in common tasks go together.

An *avant-garde* of God's design is emerging—pastors and people who willingly acknowledge Christ's lordship in every area of life. They are unwilling to equate "church" with buildings or institutional programs. They refuse to divide life into sacred and secular realms, but insist that God invades all areas of life, thought, and work. They are weary of religious hibernation and impatient with Christians who play it cool. Getting by with it, swindler-like, is not their heart's desire. Rather, getting *with it* forces them to live daringly out on a limb as Christ's ambassadors.

Technically, the *avant-garde* are persons in any art form who create original designs, advance daring ideas, and experiment with colors and forms. They are the innovators during a particular period. If they appear as rebels to traditional minds, they are willing to take that risk. For example, in Cali, Colombia, where Baptist missionaries have served since 1940, evangelicals had failed to reach university students and members of the emerging middle class. Missionary James Giles, an ethics professor, conceived the idea of a Christian Cultural Center, located adjacent to the University of the Valle campus. The center is not a "church" in the traditional sense, yet worship, religious education, and counseling are vital aspects of its mission. There are, in addition, courses in English, culinary arts, and family living. A reading room, containing copies of religious books, textbooks, periodicals, and so on, is open each day. Musical concerts, art displays, forums on current events, and guest speakers are featured periodically.

The cultural center sponsored a student retreat one weekend with more than fifty participants. George, a nominal Catholic and brilliant student—the acknowledged leader of Colombia's student social movement—professed his faith in Christ during the retreat. The following week George was offered a scholarship by Communist leaders to study at Moscow University. He declined their offer, preferring to work as a Christian leader for the betterment of his people.

By using the phrase "breaking the organizational barrier" I want to imply not rejection of the church but committed service—love in action—through traditional and new channels. Renewal through prayer, Bible study, and dialogue with fellow believers should encourage laymen to face life, to be agents of God's reconciliation where they live and work.

What can a layman do to help a church break out of its walls? I have already suggested in chaper 1 that he must take Jesus Christ seriously. If, in the spirit of Matthew 5:1-16, a layman desires purity of heart, hungers for righteousness, and reconciles enemies as a peacemaker, he cannot conceal his identity. Jesus said that the genuine disciple must live as a shining light before men "that they may see your good works and give glory to your Father who is in heaven."

Christians must decide where today's great battles are

being fought—lost or won. Struggles between forces of evil and righteousness are evident in personal and social life. Christ sends his agents of reconciliation to front-line assignments, or to change the metaphor, he seeks harvests in many fields. How can one be a reconciler in a world where meaninglessness prevails, where there is cold war strife, racial injustice, and economic privation? What about the tragic gap between the generations—the one that students feel when they go home for a holiday visit? The biggest barrier you may have to cross is not organized religion but indifference and cowardice. Select the nearest beachhead and send yourself in for a landing. Action requires the courage to change!

Good religion makes good sense. Healthy faith provides unity and structure for life's advance, step by step. Healthy laymen experience inner tensions and obvious contradictions, but they are sustained by an inner serenity. They have obtained the inheritance of a rich deposit of faith in the God of Abraham and Father of our Lord Jesus Christ.

The emergent new layman can face his growing pains and pilgrimage with full confidence in the pattern for life provided by his Lord. Through work and waiting and worship, God's faithful servant entrusts himself to an unknown future in assured hope. He admits that old landmarks are disappearing and that daily living in an open situation is risky business. New moralities may appear. New patterns of life and work are being born. Yet, in his better moments, the true layman knows that he is free only to obey, or to disobey, God. At heart, he cares.

3

Caring Is Personal

The mind of Christ has been misinterpreted by friends and foes alike. After visiting a cathedral, former Soviet Premier Khrushchev contrasted his views of life with those of Jesus Christ.

There is much in Christ that is in common with us Communists, but I cannot agree with him when he says when you are hit on the right cheek turn the left cheek. I believe in another principle. If I am hit on the left cheek I hit back on the right cheek so hard that the head might fall off. This is my sole difference with Christ.

It is true that Communist leaders destroy their enemies and Jesus sought to transform foes into friends. But Khrushchev was wrong. Revenge is not the only distinction between followers of Karl Marx and Jesus Christ. Christianity is more than a set of lofty ideals; it is a way of life. The fundamental difference between Communists and Christians is a yoke of slavery versus freedom in Christ (Gal. 5:1).

The test of Christianity is in the living—not to kill but to care.

Make Christ Your Aim

By definition the church is a fellowship (*koinōnia*) composed of individuals (1) who recognize Christ as Saviour, (2) who form durable relationships with one another, and (3) who genuinely care what happens to one another. Each local expression of the body of Christ is both a spiritual fellowship and a human community. A true congregation seeks to strengthen its members and to express Christ's concern for outsiders, as Ephesians 4:11-12 makes clear. Whatever one's occupation and avocations, his basic calling is to be a minister of Christ's redemptive mission in the world.

Because its members are fully human, however, the church is subject to error and failure. Some Christians have gifts for aiding persons that others do not possess. Because they are insecure and defensive, for example, certain members feel that other persons react negatively to them. In fact, this is frequently the case. But such a person's care may take varied forms: administration, library service, building maintenance, child supervision, and record-keeping. The intent is that one's talents be employed usefully. There is no limit to the areas in which one can express concern.

Taking Christ seriously involves making love one's aim for the sake of others (1 Cor. 14:1). Such a lofty ideal points a finger at our pious and not-so-pious pretensions. I once knew a man in the early years of automotive air-conditioning who drove through his community, in the heat of summer, with all the car windows closed. "I can't afford an air-conditioned automobile," he confided to a friend, "but people will think that I can." We would call that churchman a fraud, and his hypocrisy reminds us that churches are not immune from mask-wearing. People can also pretend to care.

Peter de Vries, in *The Mackerel Plaza*, portrays the fundamental dishonesty of a fashionable Connecticut congregation called "People's Liberal." Reverend Andrew Mackerel, the pastor, dresses smartly and mixes well with his members. Unfortunately, he does not believe in God. People's Liberal advertises itself as "a church designed to meet the needs of today, and to serve the whole man. This includes the worship of God free of outmoded theological definitions and palatable to a mind come of age in the era of Relativity." [1]

While this caricature of an imaginary church exaggerates the many subversions of the Christian mission today, we should not miss the point. Outside the church, culture masquerades as sophisticated, untouched by sin and shock, and generous toward the underdog. Inside the church, extending the "right hand of fellowship" and exchanging chitchat at the close of the Sunday morning worship period has been equated with service.

Some people evade their religious obligations by paying a trained minister to express compassion to others for them. Yet the minister cannot *do it* for you or me since Christianity is a profoundly personal affair.

How, then, may Christ become one's aim? What were the goals of his ministry? Simon Peter summarized his career thus: "He went about doing good and healing all that were oppressed by the devil, for God was with him" (Acts 10:38). Jesus himself declared that service is the key to true greatness (Mark 10:43-44) and demonstrated this unifying principle in all his relationships to persons in need (Matt. 8:28-34; Mark 5:1-20; Luke 19:10; John 13:1-16). The Jews protested his attentiveness to the disreputable, neglected members of society. His disciples were taught to translate professions of love into deeds of service which God would reward (John 21:15-17; Matt. 10:42).

The parable recorded in Matthew 25:31-46 has no parallel elsewhere in the Gospels. Two classes of persons are contrasted in Jesus' picture of the last judgment—the generous and the greedy, those who serve others and those content to save themselves. Those who were generous toward the world's insignificant, suffering people were invited into a blessed inheritance. Individuals who failed to minister to human needs departed from God's presence to "eternal punishment." Both groups were surprised to hear God's judgment.

These caring activities are the old threads that must be woven into new patterns today. Mission actions of witness and ministry require involvement in human relationships (Rom. 12:4-5) with Christian objectives in mind. Earth's sufferers need more than our good luck wishes or mere tears of sympathy. "How may a layman like myself learn to minister to others?" you may wonder, feeling that you are lucky to care for yourself and family. Personal guidance can be given to laymen who serve in such ways through pastoral instruction, group dialogue, reading, and experience. Leadership training departments can provide in-service supervision of one's work. Therefore, you need not wait until you are an accomplished worker to begin.

The above tasks merge into one another at the personal level, so radical distinctions should not be made among them. Witnessing, for example, is more than a revival effort or church membership campaign. My first teacher of evangelism in the seminary mistakenly viewed soul-winning as a special spiritual activity. We memorized one hundred selected Bible verses to "use on" various prospective members, including atheists. He proposed special techniques for entering and leaving a house or apartment, for countering objections, and for closing one's visit. Such selling tactics frequently fail to take seriously the value systems, doubts, guilt feelings, and anxieties of outsiders. Experience has taught me that God can use anything redemptive we do or say to influence persons toward Christ as Saviour. Thus, we should rely upon the Holy Spirit to make each contact with persons vital.

A man sitting across the aisle from me on a jet plane had been talking loudly about a tour he took through the mountains with his family. Punctuating with profanity his description of driving near the edge of sheer cliffs, he claimed the attention of several passengers. Momentarily he was quiet, then asked me: "By the way, what do you do . . . what is your business?" I explained that I taught in a theological school. Suddenly, he shifted subjects and shared himself at a more intimate level. He was an attorney, had been defeated as a candidate for governor during a recent primary, and was having some second thoughts about life. Can Christ use a conversation like that for his saving purpose? I am sure that he can.

Christian concern [2] is not merely an activity like teaching, calling, and counseling. It is a fundamental attitude or disposition motivated by the love of God and needs of persons. It is a matter of *being*, of risking oneself even in alien relationships, then of *doing* something constructive for one's neighbor. This implies mutual concern of Christians for one another and for those in the world for whom Christ died. Care for others that is rooted in the gospel is neither domineering nor solicitous, patronizing nor full of anxiety. It is not excessive care (*i.e.*, control) but love for others as one has been loved by God in Christ (1 John 4:18-21).

Christian Response to Human Need

A contemporary actor being interviewed by a journalist spoke of his attitude toward his audience and people in general. "Love? I don't love humanity. I don't hate them either. I just don't know them personally." Even in the make-believe world of movies this actor recognized the impossibility of loving someone he did not know. One recalls the description of a famous preacher from a past generation who loved the "world" so much that he loved no one in particular.

Christian concern, to the contrary, is never satisfactory until it becomes personal.

Concern is no secondhand affair. Christians care because God cares for persons in need. Here is a personal account of how a congregation's love became the turning

point in a young man's life. The youth faced a charge of
involuntary manslaughter following the fatal injury of a
child in an automobile accident. A prison sentence of
several years, plus a heavy fine, were the dim prospects of
his future.

One day in court changed his outlook on life. Joe was
certain that he would be found guilty when all the evidence was presented to the jury. Fortunately, Joe's pastor
and a dozen of his fellow church members joined him and
his family in the courtroom. They had driven 250 miles to
testify in his behalf as character witnesses. Although the
court found Joe guilty, he was placed on five-year proba-
tion because his friends had acted in his interest.

That evening the youth voiced his appreciation to his
pastor: "I guess I owe a lot of people a whole lot of
thanks." The minister agreed that God had worked
through the character witnesses. "That jury gave you a
second chance in life. . . . Just because all this is over," he
assured Joe, "don't think that we aren't anxious to help
you in any way possible. So feel free to call on any of us."

Did Joe's pastor or fellow church members care in order
to get something from Joe or to gain control of his life?
No. The only logic behind such costly concern is Christian
agape—a Greek word for sacrificial love. That word, implying self-giving responsibility for the "other," abounds
in the New Testament. John 3:16 uses it to describe God
as love and the sacrifice of Christ on the cross as his
supreme act of love. Agape love assumes responsibility for
another person or group even at great risk and cost to
oneself.

We can see from this that agape love is more than an emotion, whim, feeling, or temporary mood. Love seeks an object and serves a purpose in its expression—the welfare of some person or group. Thus, Christ's hand was God's healing touch, his voice was God's perfect wisdom, and his death was God's adequate sacrifice for human redemption. What Jesus did was never satisfactory until it became personal. He called himself the true shepherd who knew his flock and sacrificed himself for his sheep (John 10:11-14).

Response is personal. A pastor of a metropolitan congregation numbering several thousand members once was questioned by a friend: "How many members of your congregation do you know personally?" Reflecting momentarily, the minister who had preached many years in that place replied: "I suppose I know 500 persons intimately. The rest are casual acquaintances, some of whom I know by name only." Caring for persons in a secular world requires both profound wisdom and personal intimacy in those who would communicate with them about God's healing power.

Contrast the pastor's testimony with that of a Christian psychiatrist who practiced medicine in New York City. "You are in the business of teaching ministers to care for people," he said as a guest in a theological faculty seminar. "How many people can you love at one time. . . . I mean investing intensively in their lives, sharing their pilgrimage?" The seminary professors fumbled for a suitable answer.

The physician supplied his own answer. "I limit my

practice of intensive psychotherapy to five persons at any given time. There is no way for me to cope effectively with all the sad worlds of all the shaken people who desire appointments with me. You see," he explained, "I've learned how much one man can carry of other people's loads. And I can love only five people adequately at once." Of course, he taught psychiatry in a medical school, functioned actively as a deacon in his church, was a family man, and counseled several hundred patients each year.

What does this man's discovery imply about a person like yourself who volunteers his talents in the life of the church? *First, that everybody has relationships.* Since concern is no secondhand affair, you can start where you are and witness to what Christ means in your own life. You do not have to wait for some survey of special needs or specialists to project a program in your community. While Peace Corps members receive unique training for the country in which they shall serve, they permit nothing to obscure the significance of individual relationships with nationals.

Second, we ought to stay alert to how persons around us suffer and are threatened in daily existence. Persons are hurt by sin, rebellion against God, the influence of human idolatries. They suffer rivalry within the family, conflicts, and misunderstanding at the hands of persons who know them best. The privacy of existence is invaded by sickness, accidents, delinquency, social conflict, acts of terrorism and inhumanity, and unfavorable economic circumstances. Our entire world is struggling amid resurgent nationalism, party strife, Communist advance, and hatred between whites and people of color. We are each subject to acts of nature: hail, earthquakes, and violent storms.

You may be able to help someone with whom you have a relationship: parent-child, teacher-student, pastor-church member, employer-employee, and so on. Helpers themselves are frequently in need of healing or encouragement. Hence, *care* is not a one-way street but a complex expressway, including bridges and interchanges. Certainly united efforts, sometimes including the aid of specialists, are necessary.

Barriers to Concern

Like the priest and the Levite in Jesus' parable of the good Samaritan, our human tendency is to view wounded spirits from a safe distance. Through secret indifference and desire for self-preservation people answer no to the cry for help. "We are all too busy to be neighborly," someone reasons. Busy doing what—going nowhere fast? To what shall we attribute this preference to preserve one's own ego, to look out for oneself?

1. One barrier to concern is selfishness or egocentricity. People get caught up in momentary, secular pleasures. They forget God. For example, some clergymen interviewed twenty young men and women in Dallas—apartment dwellers who enjoyed a self-contained existence in the midst of cocktail parties, the swimming pool, and luxurious surroundings.

"I used to go to church regularly—Congregationalist—even through college," confided a tall dental hygienist.

"But I haven't been since I started living here." Her date, a real-estate salesman who also lived in the apartment complex, said he had gone to church as a boy but had stopped regular attendance when he went to college. "It was a church-related university," he explained. "I was taking religion three days a week, so I figured I could skip Sundays. The upshot is that now I hardly go to church at all." How can indifferent young adults who have quit the church bear the burdens of their friends? Some of them do and testify that they have experienced mutually satisfying relationships beyond the church's influence.

2. Some people lack confidence. They avoid threats to their own security system. Perhaps they feel inadequate to cope with their own personal or family problems, much less to aid other troubled people. Anxiety and guilt over poor education that ill-equipped them for life forces many people into silence. They think special "techniques" have to be learned and used in pastoral care. Primarily, it is Christ himself who helps and heals through persons who speak the truth in love (Eph. 4:15). Because caring skills are essential, however, they will be discussed in chapter 4.

3. A sagging self-esteem restricts the helping ministries of pastors and laymen alike. Here is a father, for example, whose authority has been reduced considerably since his sixteen-year-old daughter was forced to marry because of pregnancy out of wedlock. A pastor may have counseled many hours with some estranged marriage partners in an effort to save their home. Then he learns that they divorced despite his efforts. Such churchmen may wonder, "What's the use?"

A major adjustment of young physicians is learning to accept many failures in their treatment efforts. Not all of their patients will improve. Some will die. Accepting a "lower therapeutic ambition" (*i.e.*, many failures) is not easy but is necessary in the helping professions. The physician's training in science forces him to reevaluate constantly all treatment efforts—successes and failures. Perhaps people who care in the church can learn from the professional habits of physicians and thereby improve their skills.

4. Fear over the consequences of involvement in another person's problem, or in a public controversy, stills the hands of would-be helpers. The temptation to play it safe, be quiet, to conform to what is expected, cautions us. Ordinary people want to be left alone, to avoid trouble.

You will recall that the Jewish authorities in Jesus' day warned him that religion and politics don't mix. The powers that be said there would be trouble if he kept on stirring up the people. Eventually his involvement with sinful mankind led Christ to Calvary.

Fear is a real emotion in our lives. Once while riding a train I talked with a Pullman porter about some important issues of the day. When the conversation turned to race relations he became especially cautious. "I'd be glad to discuss the subject with you sometime when I'm off the job," he explained, "because I have my views. But it's a company policy. They just don't want no trouble." Rank and file Americans want to stay in good standing with persons in authority: union bosses, the law, work supervisors, the church crowd, and powerful politicians.

Automobile drivers are warned by safety experts not to offer rides to hitchhikers. "A person making a journey today should have funds for some sort of transportation: bus, train, or plane," goes the argument. They do well to warn us, for some nice, agreeable people have been robbed, kidnapped, beaten, even raped by calloused villains whom they befriended. Admittedly, it is difficult to study a situation in the context of the love of God when someone is in jeopardy or great temptation. Fools still rush in "where angels fear to tread."

Healthy fear of or at least respect for some sticky situations and types of people should caution Christian involvement. For example, I know a minister who became acutely aware of the problems of illness because of a handicapped child in his own home. Like a physician, he wanted health for everyone. Thus, when an influenza epidemic struck many households in his community, the pastor assisted health authorities with drug injections. But his urge to help cost him his job. Some thoughtless parishioners rumored that their minister was addicted to drugs. He had been seen with syringes and needles and was suspected of injecting himself with drugs. The congregation voted to discharge him without appraisal of the actual situation. *That* is the reverse of true concern.

To summarize, indifference, insecurity, introversion, and fear of involvement seal our eyes to potential objects of love. Opportunities for helping people are all about us, and Christians need to care. What we need is not a new gospel but the combined resources of persons like yourself directed toward redemptive objectives.

4

Increasing Caring Skills

By now you may be recalling varied persons for whom you lacked the courage to care, such as (1) an aged parent who died feeling unloved, (2) a newcomer in your residential area whom you failed to welcome, (3) a business associate who was denied the radiance of your Christian testimony, (4) a child who might have flowered in the warmth of your friendship, or (5) a debtor whom you failed to forgive. The older we grow the more we realize that some goals will never be accomplished. Disappointments and deficiencies are marked, not unfeelingly, into the diaries of our daily lives.

Some failures appear to be final, such as turning from marriage to divorce or from legitimate ambition to delinquent behavior, rebelling against one's own people, expressing racial prejudice, or abandoning a position for which one has worked all his life. These, at heart, are failures in relationships that cannot be easily explained. Yet failure may not be the end, but the beginning of a new phase of development. A psychiatrist encouraged a patient thus: "Your nervous 'breakdown' was actually a 'breakthrough' into new freedom and authentic existence."

Kierkegaard, Danish philosopher of the last century, once observed about Christians: "In his failure the believer finds his triumph." This was true of the apostle Paul who, though persecuted, confessed: "I want you to know, brethren, that what has happened to me has really served to advance the gospel" (Phil. 1:12). So often we learn best not by winning but by losing. Thus God can carve out a new channel in which one's life may flow toward the immortal sea of his divine purpose. One who has been comforted by God's Spirit can never doubt the grace that claims him, though his life is spent in greater mystery.

You recall the qualities of caring persons mentioned thus far: (1) agape love, (2) sensitivity to human needs, (3) a gift to give, (4) inner serenity as the token of victory over suffering, and (5) the peace of God, by which we have been comforted in our own failures and grief experiences. These marks of maturity are relative achievements in Christian experience—goals toward which we strive. Browning was right: "A man's reach must exceed his grasp."

Are You Available?

One pastor I know spends about twenty-five hours each week in diligent sermon preparation. He preaches well-polished messages, containing numerous quotations and apt illustrations. But he visits rarely with people in or outside the church. In fact, he is contacted only in emergencies which staff members cannot handle.

Is there anything wrong with having a little privacy, whether at work or at home, you ask? Definitely not. You must have some time alone for personal grooming, spiritual growth, private conversations, needed rest, and creative labor.

I am speaking here, however, of the skill of accessibility—making oneself available to family members, fellow workers, students, clients, colleagues, patients, or church members. While there is room for all kinds of persons in the ministry, including the scholarly recluse, there is also a *need for a presence*—a pastor who cares for people—in our churches.

Protestant pastors often feel caught in a professional trap. There are sermons to prepare, sick folk to visit, prospective members to enlist, civic affairs to support, bulletins to compose, reports to submit, committees to attend, *plus* anxiety over inadequacy, guilt over failure, hostility toward criticism, and never enough time. The wife of a downtown minister said during a Wednesday night dinner at church: "My husband and I have had dinner together alone only one time this entire month." One is reminded of the wisdom of the comic strip character Pogo who said: "We have met the enemy. They is us!"

Pastors and people can be too busy at church to deal with vital issues. God does not require our "busyness," only our faithfulness in living the gospel wherever we are. We must continually break out of institutional modes of thinking into personal and small group relationships.

Finding more time to be available to persons in need is a problem for laymen, not just ministers. For example, a patient in psychotherapy, paying $35.00 a visit, became discouraged when her psychiatrist kept falling asleep dur-

ing counseling sessions. Thinking that he was tired at 4:00
P.M. each Thursday—her hour—she rescheduled appointments at 10:00 A.M., earlier in the week. But, to her dis-
may, the therapist still napped while she poured out
disappointments, snags, and failures in her developmental
history.

"Was she a bore?" you may wonder, or "Was the doctor
a tired old man?" Whatever the answer, that professional
"caretaker" in accepting a client entered a covenant of
faithfulness with her to strengthen insight and responsibility. She felt rejected, and rightly so, because the door of
his soul (not his office) appeared closed.

To open oneself *in Christ's spirit* to a neighbor's spiritual lostness, moral confusion, shattering crisis, or social
want can be a costly action. Such openness is spontaneous,
for generosity cannot be programed. A popular songwriter
has given contemporary expression to an ancient longing:
"What the world needs now is love, sweet love." But one
has to like people, and be secure himself, to risk redemptive relationships.

How can others know that you are there and that you
care—in family relationships, for example?

Parents can increase their accessibility to their own children by spending some time during the week (daily if
possible) with each of them. Most young parents want to
get away from their children and let the baby-sitter take
over. God gave children two parents for a purpose. They
need a father—a masculine person with whom to identify—as well as a mother. A growing child looks upon
adults as all-powerful, mysteriously wise, and financially

stable. Of course, they shed such illusions in adolescence and see the inconsistencies and human flaws in both parents. Still, boys and girls like to talk with grown-ups about many things: God, the world, animals, their brothers and sisters, school, sex, even the characters in their favorite bedtime stories.

Care Requires Involvement

Already, you see that accessibility is more a matter of spirit, a helpful disposition, than of sitting in an office waiting for a knock on the door. Care takes the initiative, makes a call, sees a need, and acts on a generous impulse to help. Consider the following example.

An elementary schoolteacher who worked with socially deprived children was riding home from work one afternoon with her husband. "Charles," she said, "I want to run by Rich's and buy little Sherry some casual shoes."

"Sherry who?" he replied.

"You know! She's one of the youngsters from the Hope Children's Home who was transferred to my room in January."

"Those kids are always needing something," Charles answered disgustedly. "They're either sick, or in some kind of trouble. I wish you wouldn't get involved with them!"

Do Christians have a right to avoid getting "involved" with people in trouble? Christ was always "taking a towel and girding himself" in order to minister to others and to set an example for believers. Just as he preached "deliverance to the captives" in the days of his flesh, he works through Christians in order to bring hope to men today. That elementary teacher knew the plight of a child who needed shoes like the others in her classroom had. So she purchased them and presented them in a moment of privacy to a youngster trapped by the divorce of parents, neither of whom wanted her.

How different this disposition is from that of laymen who expect favors from friends, or ministers who know someone that can "get it for them wholesale."

Along with incidental, casual, and spontaneous opportunities for service, churches will plan specific ways to meet varied needs. Planned mission activities may touch lives of outsiders: a racial minority, socially disadvantaged families, patients in a mental hospital, residents of a convalescent home, or physically handicapped citizens like the deaf. On mission fields classes are offered in culinary arts, home nursing, child care, sanitation, literacy, and varied crafts, as well as Bible study. Special programs, with pastoral intent, may be conducted with persons or groups in the church.

One church planned a "cues for college" day for all graduating high school seniors. It was a guidance program of orientation in a recreation center which afforded decorative surroundings, a delicious luncheon, and swimming privileges in addition to four dialogue sessions. The basic purpose of the effort was to expose students planning to attend college to the academic, social, and religious atmosphere of the modern campus, under the direction of capable Christian educators. Imagine the sense of significance that those young people experienced as they talked with top personnel about varied areas of college life. Fears and frustrations came out in the small groups. Information displaced illusions. The promise of monthly mailings of a Christian student publication[1] and pledge of friendship from adults in the educational power structure encouraged all of the participants. Each student appreciated the opportunity.

It will take several years to evaluate the effectiveness of such efforts, but the initial response of students and staff was excellent.

Communicating Concern

Assuming your willingness to risk encounters with alien persons—to be accessible—how can a layman build bridges between the church and the world? Personal piety is honorable, but being merely a proper Christian is inadequate when one sees his neighbors fighting for status and success, or trapped by poverty, or injured by cruel social forces. We must not be indifferent when crises come. People are weak and need God's help. The best way to learn what their real needs are is by listening and responding to the facts and feelings they express.

For example, Howard West, a barber shop owner, once shared a family grief experience with one of his employees. Howard's son Max and daughter-in-law, Doris, had a baby son born with a congenital heart defect. This was the Wests's first grandchild, born with only half a heart. Kirk died within six weeks after birth, and the Wests were plunged into grief for themselves and their son.

About a month after the infant grandson's death, the

family entertained Bud, one of Mr. West's employees, for dinner. According to Bud, the following is a partial account of their conversation after the evening meal. (To help our insight, let us put this in the form of a dramatic play.)

Bud inquired about Max and Doris. Mrs. West brought in some pictures of little Kirk, then returned to the dishes in the kitchen. Howard spoke first.

HOWARD: Doesn't he look good? You would never guess that he had a sick day in in his life. (*Note his grandfatherly pride.*)

BUD (*the employee*): He really does look healthy. (*Shortly, Mrs. West returned to talk with them.*)

MRS. WEST: Doesn't the baby look sweet?

BUD: Yes, he does. He looks like a normal healthy baby, as I just told Howard.

MRS. WEST: Well, he acted healthy, too. He would kick and move about in the incubator. He was really active to be so sick. It was nice of you men at the shop to send flowers to the service. Here are some of the beautiful flowers that people sent. Aren't they pretty? (*The room was crowded with pot plants.*)

BUD: Yes, they are. (*Mrs. West spoke of Doris and of people's kindnesses.*)

BUD: I suppose Max and Doris are about settled down from this experience.

MRS. WEST: Well, of course, Max is right back in the groove of school, and I suppose Doris has become adjusted to it also. Really, we are all just now getting out from under the pressure of it. It was so very hard for awhile. Howard and I would talk about little Kirk every day, wouldn't we, Howard?

HOWARD: Yes, we would. But we decided that we would have

to stop living in the past. I guess you call it that, don't you? It doesn't bother us to talk about it now. It was just one of those things you would like to forget. At least, we don't think about it all of the time.

BUD: Do you think that there was purpose in it all? What I mean is, do you think that it happened for any particular reason?

MRS. WEST: Well, my minister said there was a reason.

HOWARD: Of course, we can't see why or the reason now. Maybe later we will. We first thought that perhaps it was because Max was still in school and a child would just have been another burden on them. But we felt also that the loss of a child would be a heavier burden, so that idea really didn't make sense to us. We now feel like this is all what God wanted and that it is all for the best.

MRS. WEST: What's the Scripture verse in Romans that Brother Polk (*their minister*) read to us?

HOWARD: I don't remember. It's something about everything is for the best to the children of God. Do you know what verse it might be, Bud?

BUD: Yes, I know that verse. 'All things work for the good of them that love the Lord' (*Rom. 8:28*).

HOWARD: Yes, that's it. That's all we can say now.

MRS. WEST: Isn't it wonderful how one verse like that can set your mind at ease?

BUD: Yes, it is wonderful. That's the power of God's Word. It is always sufficient for our every need.

HOWARD: Well, I know one thing. This experience has taught me how weak we are and how much we need other people. You really discover who your friends are when something like this happens.

MRS. WEST: You sure do. And another thing, Max and Doris have been to church together every Sunday since the funeral. He used not to go because he needed to study. At least they go to the morning services now.

BUD: You are seeing some purpose in it already.

HOWARD: You just never know, do you? I mean, this thing is so
rare. The doctor said that only one out of every ten or
twenty thousand births occur with this type of heart defect.
There must be a real good reason for those odds to fall on
us. You just never know.

MRS. WEST: But we do know that God loves his children. He
knew it would be better to take little Kirk home than to let
him suffer so much here on earth.

BUD: Yes, that's right. God doesn't like to see any of us suffer.
(*Thereafter, the conversation drifted off to other areas,
news affairs, and so on.*)

Later, in reflecting upon the conversation, Bud noted
his anxiety about using religious jargon with the Wests.
He was afraid to "talk spiritual," as he put it. Yet, God's
Spirit was evident during their visit. Howard and his wife
spoke freely of their grief and disappointment precisely
because their guest was a good listener. This family was
independent and resourceful. Yet they discovered that,
upon occasion, people need other people and God desper-
ately. When the matter of *purpose* was mentioned, the
Wests clarified what their gains—human and divine—
from the experience had been. True, Bud did not say
much, but what he said supported the Wests' disrupted
value system and permitted them to verbalize God's revelation through the death experience.

Can you enhance your capacity as an understanding
Christian communicator? What can be learned from clini-
cal evidence in the above visit?

1. You may have little control over an interview, for

you talk with numerous people every day. As in Bud's case, you can counsel persons with whom you have a relationship of mutual trust and confidence. On the other hand, some people find it easier to talk with a stranger than with a close friend. You may have an opportunity to be that stranger.

2. Therapeutic (healing) conversations cannot be forced upon a "prospect." You can take the initiative by making yourself available to another person, but he must desire to share himself with you in the presence of God.

3. The time and place of your conversation should afford privacy, emotional freedom, and unhurried affection for the person or family. A physician, for example, who is related formally to his patients will talk with them in an office setting. But you, a friend making an informal visit, may talk with persons in a house or wayside place such as a store.

4. You may not have all the answers. Bud's role was that of a Christian friend and employee. He did not "play God" by aggressively controlling the conversation, voicing judgment upon Max and Doris for poor church attendance, or explaining why Kirk died. He disavowed the role of a judge or a minister in favor of the role of friend.

5. Bud did not try to carry the Wests's burdens for them. In the spirit of Galatians 6:1-5, he shared their burdens and transferred their dependency needs to God, from whom our help comes (cf. Psalm 121:1-4). This is true pastoral care in that the individual or family is permitted to grow through suffering in the power of God's Spirit.

Along with these lessons about communicating concern, here are some guidelines for laymen to follow in counseling experiences. They are listed without comment because their meaning is clear.

(1) Prepare your heart properly through prayer in order to present God to an individual or family in need.

(2) Respect the counselee. Be interested in him as a person, not just curious about his problem.

(3) Consider the problem as important. Don't belittle or mock an individual, regardless of the problem's nature.

(4) Remember that suffering people are sensitive, often hostile; be patient no matter how superficial, halting, or shocking the story.

(5) Resist the temptation to pry into unrevealed secrets.

(6) Let the counselee use his words, assume responsibility for his actions, and make his own decisions.

(7) Be willing to admit that you do not have or need to have all of the answers.

(8) Explore acceptable alternatives without attempting to convert a person to your point of view. Of course, in evangelistic visitation, you will keep the conversation Christ-centered, using appropriate Scripture passages.

(9) Watch your spirit! Try not to be defensive or argumentative in response to the person's words or basic attitudes. It is easy to become impatient or abrupt.

(10) Walk alongside the person until a course of action is settled upon, or make additional time for another interview if that seems necessary.

Listening and responding to facts or feelings of other

people is not an inherited quality. Sharing another's plight and pilgrimage is a learned experience. Some people need a course in remedial listening. Others should practice keeping confidences. Do not expect someone to bare his soul, share secret sins or hurts, unless you intend to share something of yourself. *Your interest and comradely care will prove more effective than giving advice or rejecting a worrier.*

Visiting Is Witnessing Too

Some people spend their lives preparing to live, intending to serve God and mankind. They never plunge into the adventure.[2] Like the character in Russell H. Conwell's famous story *Acres of Diamonds,* some persons think that if they were living in some other place, or had entered another vocation, they would have more success. You may recall that the man sold his farm and sought his fortune out in the world. In time, the farm's new owner discovered tiny stones shimmering in the sun—stones that later proved to be diamonds. Had the original owner looked carefully at his opportunity he would have possessed a fortune in gems.

Visiting is like that. The layman who waits for "one shining moment in history" to testify of his faith in God will likely never visit in the church's behalf. There is much to be said for a social call which is simply a friendly visit with a neighbor or newly arrived family in your city. Not every visit will be devoted to discussing theology, the church, or personal problems. You don't have to look for trouble when calling in Christ's name.

Take the case of a lady who began visiting women in the local jail, then started a Bible class for inmates.[3] "Reading my Bible sent me scurrying to jail!" confessed Mrs. Warner E. Fusselle. "The words I read were the words of Jesus: 'I was sick, and you visited me, I was in prison and you came to me'" (Matt. 25:36). She took Christ seriously.

Recalling her early impressions of the county jail, Mrs. Fusselle described the bare floors, bleak walls, barred windows, lonely cells, and the unsavory-looking characters around and in the jail. She was more impressed, however, with female prisoners who spent weary days on their bunks. Only a spoon was permitted for eating. No furniture was permitted except the iron bunks. The prisoners' faces bore horrible signs of bitterness and sin. One woman, about forty, had a scar on her forehead and tattoos on each arm. There were drug addicts, alcoholics, prostitutes, and first offenders, including one girl who was pregnant out of wedlock.

The Christian visitor taught them Bible lessons each Monday, carried them literature, food, her love, and her Saviour. She was attracted to the unwed, expectant mother who said that she wanted to keep her baby. "I want one thing that is really mine to love. My father ruined me because of drink. My mother would not believe me. After that I never cared what happened." Later, she admitted that adoption was best but asked that the infant be placed with a nondrinking couple.

Mrs. Fusselle confessed that she had never had any training or experience to prepare her for work in a jail. "I do not like, humanly speaking, to visit the jail. But I love the Saviour. I want to follow his footsteps wherever they may lead me. I have found that people in jail are just people, too. They are people who need to know the Saviour."

We may conclude that loving interest in and concern for people is the basic purpose for church visitation. There may or may not be a major crisis. Yet, even in social calls, you should have a reason for calling and trust God's Spirit to prepare the way for a redemptive relationship.

Successful visitors can help the beginner to avoid superficial contacts and wasted trips. Specific guidance for hospital calling will be provided in chapter 7. Here are some guidelines for visiting persons with pastoral intent.

1. By carrying the church to people, you are free to meet them on their own ground, see them in the context of daily experience, and understand their outlook upon life.

2. Prepare for calling by checking areas of the city in which you accepted an address or assignment. Apartment addresses can be especially confusing when several buildings that look alike are clustered together.

3. A time for visiting will be determined by your own schedule and that of the person with whom you shall get acquainted. Some visitors call in advance, not just to make an appointment, but to make certain the family or party will be at home.

4. While company in calling—like your wife, a deacon, or staff member—is not essential, it is often helpful. Two separate pictures of a situation are obtained. One caller offsets the errors or impatience of another visitor. Some

potential church members will admit a couple into a house or apartment but would refuse admittance to a single man.

5. Begin graciously with the person for his own sake. Have a kind word about the family, a floral arrangement, or the house. Get to know the person by listening to his religious background, family interests, work concerns, hobbies, and so on. Circumstances will dictate whether or not you should use the Bible and prayer. Stay long enough to accomplish your purpose, but do not prolong the discussion. If records are desired by your church office, these should be provided for the sake of other visitors who follow you.

Someone may reason that visitation is the pastor's job. You may hear a fellow church member say: "That's what we're paying Harry to do." It is likely that the total task of pastoral care of all the church's members and prospective members will exceed the capacities of both pastor and staff. You may share the age-old task of calling upon newcomers, the sick, aged, shut-ins, nonmembers, and bereaved persons for the glory of God.

Praying for Others

Many church members feel so helpless when news comes of persons in need. They obtain information but fail to act. This feeling about one's involvement in crucial situations has already led us to a consideration of what one person like yourself can do: make yourself available, understand through conversations, and dare to witness through visitation.

Logically, we come now to consider how prayer can help others.

The New Testament makes much of the practice of prayer in behalf of persons in need. Portions of our Lord's prayers are threaded into the Gospels (Matt. 6:9-13; John 17). He instructed his disciples to pray privately, not publicly as did the hypocritical Jews (Matt. 6:6). Jesus spent long hours in communion with his Heavenly Father (Mark 1:35, 6:46; Luke 5:15, 6:12). In the garden of Gethsemane Christ pleaded that, if it were his Father's will, the cup of suffering might be withdrawn (Luke 22:42).

Some moderns think that prayer—vital communion with God, who has spoken to us in printed and living Word—is a waste of time. They conclude that God has predestined all things to happen, so why pray? From man's side, prayer appears to be his effort to release resources in his behalf which are beyond his control. Yet, from God's side, prayer is a grace gift—his promise to listen, to understand, and to act in behalf of any true believer. This is why he commanded prayer for and by the saints (1 Chron. 16:11; Hos. 14:2; Matt. 7:7; Luke 18:1; John 16:24; Eph. 6:18).

Christians have this certainty: God does answer prayer. Numerous promises of answers to prayers are found in the Scriptures. The disciples were instructed to pray in "Jesus' name"—meaning that they were to live, not merely speak, in obedience to him (Luke 11:9; John 15:7). Through obedience members of the early church were blessed by God's Spirit, and many persons were saved and healed

(Acts 1:14, 4:24; James 5:15-16). Prayer exerts an influence upon God's action, even upon his existence.[4] This is what the word "answer" means.

How does God answer us? The foundation of our prayers centers in Jesus Christ. If his words truly "abide in" us, he shall intercede continually as our high priest (Heb. 10:19-21), and we may expect God's response (1 John 3:22). This assurance increases our faith and steadies our hands for tasks that we can do. Admittedly, there is much mystery in prayer, for God remains free to act as he wills. Yet, he listens to us. John the apostle envisioned angels mingling incense with prayers, "and the smoke of the incense rose with the prayers of the saints from the hand of the angel before God" (Rev. 8:4). This is the ground of Christian assurance.

In Christ, God taught us how to pray, and through his Spirit he participates in the anxious longings and joyous thanksgiving of his children. The Holy Spirit intercedes with God himself when overwhelmed Christians do not know how to pray or what to say (Rom. 8:26).

How shall we pray? Posture in prayer makes little difference; it is the believer's attitude that counts. He must humble himself before God. We do not have to shout or use holy words. What matters is that God listens, not that our words are forceful. We must think of *him*, not preach to auditors who may overhear our words. Effective prayer is appropriate to the occasion, voluntary or spontaneous, not forced, natural in tone, and offered in a spirit of reverence.

How does prayer help? In John Baillie's words, prayer

helps us to "sense the presence of God." (1) We are to place our trust in God, *not* in our words. A woman once said to C. E. Autrey: "I've lost my faith in prayer." She explained her doubts and said that her words were not getting out of the room. "The problem," he responded, "is that you are not truly trusting God." (2) Prayer reminds us of things we have forgotten and causes us to relax our desires into greater plans than our own. (3) Prayer helps us to gain perspective. It enlarges our vision and expands our concern. (4) Prayer sensitizes us to the needs of others, as well as ourselves. We are strengthened by the fellowship of other trusting people who pray, as well as by the witness of the saints in the Bible.

You may be thinking about those dark times in your life when God heard your requests for health, or success, or family unity—yet said no. Nothing makes for disappointment more than does optimism or complacency when the conditions do not sustain it. With God "all things are possible." Yet, from the human point of view some things are impossible. God, however, answers his children in one of two ways. He answers our *request* and grants the petition; or he answers the *believer* while refusing his request. In either instance, God's true child is reinforced for life. He can say: "In his will is my peace."

There are varied ways through which the church's fellowship may be extended to persons facing life's hazards, decisions, and responsibilities that we shall not discuss. Two matters merit brief mention here, however. The first concerns your *keeping in touch through correspondence* with persons who mean much to you or who rely upon your friendship. Time and distance separate persons and families today. Yet occasions like birthdays, anniversaries, weddings, and commencements offer opportunities to express interest in friends of all ages. I know one lady who composes poetry, with a specific person or occasion in mind, then sends a copy to the honoree. Personal notes may be written in your own hand thanking friends or relatives for gifts or a visit, expressing appreciation to some civic leader or teacher, or assuring a sick friend of your concern. Where personal visits or telephone calls are impossible, with foreign missionaries for example, a message can be mailed inexpensively.

The complexity of human needs today requires consideration of a final matter—*referring persons in difficult situations to specialists* who have the education or organized resources commensurate with the problems involved. Social, medical, and public welfare resources are made available to all citizens regardless of race or religious affiliation. There are persons—delinquents, sex deviants, criminals, the severely retarded, and mentally ill—whose limitless needs can quickly overtax the resources of one person, family, or congregation.

Such situations call for a nonroutine approach, for professional experience in coping with persons in such circumstances, and for organized resources that guarantee continual, even long-term, assistance if it is required. Do not count it a "crime" or personal failure when someone's need lies beyond you. Be wise enough to consult ministers, physicians, legal aid officials, educators, and social workers who are trained to cope with desperate situations.

5

Evangelism and Encouragement

At its best the church is a community of Christians who care for one another and seek by varied means to extend that care to persons outside the church. In preceding chapters we considered the church's task of offering salvation to all men, and showed how this ministry requires the cooperative efforts of all Christians. Taking Ephesians 4:11-13 seriously, we have sought to equip the laity for Christian service. This includes witnessing in the church and in the world at large.

Man's need for reconciliation with God—to become a new being—places a priority on evangelism. The church is under Christ's orders to disciple all nations, "baptizing them in the name of the Father and of the Son and of the Holy Spirit, teaching them to observe all that [he] commanded" (Matt. 28:19-20). Christian persons who are "joint heirs of the grace of life" (1 Pet. 3:7) witness to their faith in daily relationships whether they intend to or not.

For example, Clay, a high school student, was talking with his father about his education. They discussed school subjects, teachers, and classroom procedures. "One thing about Mr. Kimball," observed Clay, "regardless of the grades you make on his tests, you know that he cares. And that makes all the difference!" Actually, Mr. Kimball communicates Christian concern *both* in the academic community where he teaches *and* in his church where he leads a boys' study group.

A common misconception is that Christian "witnesses" are career missionaries, chaplains, ministers, and so on. An ordinary layman, like yourself, preferring not to appear too religious or pious often avoids involvement in religious activities. As a result, lack of concern for lost people plagues modern churches.

Indifference is not confined to the churches. Apathy and personnel shortages also occur among nonchurch groups like civic clubs and service leagues. (Their members are our church members, too!) One city recreation planner requested that civic groups provide activity leaders for three thousand teen-agers who failed to find summer employment. The general response was: "We will do everything *short of supplying personnel* for recreation leadership." Leaders were needed, but civic-minded clubmen evaded involvement with city youth.

Some churches have rejected revivalism and evangelism, while others thrive on these, perhaps to the neglect of nurture and service. Compulsive aggressiveness for additions to church membership often parades under the guise of compassion. Some congregations appear to be closed corporations. Others reach and baptize the offspring of their present membership. While commendable, this is not enough. Perhaps church leaders are at fault. Many people neither understand the meaning of conversion nor the process of Christian witnessing.

Each Conversion Is Unique

Professional evangelists and church executives preoccupied with denominational economics and institutional gains are guilty of putting undue pressure on people in and out of the church. The major concern of Jesus Christ was not in sustaining or boosting previous records but in calling persons to faith in himself. He beckoned men to belief in different ways. We serve one Lord, but we come to him through a variety of conversion experiences.[1]

What does the biblical teaching on conversion mean for us today? John the Baptist turned to Jesus of Nazareth with a sense of obedience as prophecy was fulfilled (Mark 1:4-11). Early disciples followed him out of wonder, admiration, and a sense of expectancy (John 1:35-51). Nicodemus was amazed at his teachings (John 3:1-21). Saul (later Paul) recognized Christ as one whom he had disobeyed (Acts 9:1-19). The Philippian jailer found salvation in the midst of a great crisis (Acts 16:19-34).

Students of the Scriptures, as well as of human personality, have long recognized that one's background shapes his response to the Saviour. Some believers experience cataclysmic changes. Others, children particularly, turn gradually and serenely to Christ. The genius of conversion has to do with *depth*, not speed. As the Master himself taught us, *decision* to turn from sin (rebellion against God) and *commitment* to himself as Lord are the essentials of salvation (cf. Luke 15:3-32). Thus repentance and faith are two sides of the same coin in a convert's experience.

David Roberts once wrote that salvation is "that condition of wholeness which comes about when human life is based in openness (*i.e.*, with 'self-knowledge') upon the creative and redemptive power of God." [2] Conversion is thus a divine-human transaction reached by means of God's grace and man's freedom. It is not merely "joining the church," getting oneself baptized, or doing in copycat fashion what everyone else is doing. One who opens his life to God's healing grace in private confession, however, should desire to make a public affirmation of Christ as Saviour. Following baptism into a church's membership, the new convert grows through contacts with fellow believers and the guidance of the Holy Spirit.

Varieties of Conversion

We have said that God enters each life through a private door. No one type or method of religious experience should seek prominence over other forms. To enhance your effectiveness as a Christian witness, consider the following ways people found the Saviour and identified with his church.

1. *Some fortunate people are taught to trust Christ from childhood.* A woman talking with the new member orientation committee of her church confided: "I was reared in a home of love by Christian parents. There has never been a time in my life when I did not love Jesus." Is that mere sentimentality? No, the influence of a godly family and cultivation of a Christian conscience made her sensitive to

God at an early age. She grew up into Christ, as did Paul's young friend Timothy, counteracting temptations along the way. Conversion came through her personal surrender to Christ in preadolescent years. This may parallel your own experience.

2. *Some converts are jarred from their spiritual inactivity by tragic events or by strong feelings of unworthiness and shame.* Bruce, a young man in his late twenties, once related to a group how God had become real for him. The son of a prominent physician, he grew up enjoying some of the finer things and pleasurable experiences of life, such as music, golf, and travel. Unfortunately, his family was indifferent to the church.

"I was christened as a child," he noted, "but didn't take God seriously. Then, one day, as a college student I waked up to life. My dad called the children into his room and told us that he and mother were getting a divorce. I was stunned. It happens to other people, I thought, but why us?" Bruce felt different, cut off from the festival of life, and depressed because of the effect of his parents' divorce.

He described months of anxious longing—questions without answers—until one day at church his eyes fell upon these words of Scripture: "For by grace you have been saved through faith; and this is not your own doing, it is the gift of God—not because of works, lest any man should boast" (Eph. 2:8-9). He sought the counsel of a pastor. Following a public confession of his faith in Christ, Bruce sought the companionship of Christian friends. He struggled out of anguished depression into the joy of

Christian service. "That's the first time that I really understood what *gift* means," he concluded.

3. *A third group of believers have come to the Christian faith after yielding to great temptations.* They have been relieved of a burden of guilt through confession to God and to Christian people (cf. James 5:16-20). This was true of Augustine, you recall, and has been the case of many hardened sinners.

Some children noticed a stooped, white-haired man walking with the aid of a cane, who always attended worship services in their church. He and his aged wife, unceremoniously yet ritually, sat on the second pew from the front of the sanctuary. They were poorly dressed and seldom spoke to anyone.

"Why does Mr. Mac always sit on the second row?" asked a small boy. "He cannot hear well," replied his mother, "so he sits close to the preacher and the choir." The children pressed for additional information about the quiet old man. Their parents explained that, years before, Mr. Mac had killed a man in a moment of anger. He had experienced the judgment of God, and of society, during years of a lonely existence. Then a man befriended Mr. Mac and his family, supplying food and clothing during the great depression years. Mr. Mac came to believe, through such kindness and acceptance, that the Lord is compassionate and merciful. Through that layman's witness of practical love he responded by entrusting his life to God.

Looking for words to voice the prayer of people like Mr. Mac, they must pray something like this: "My past hide;

my future guide." God who is faithful and just hears such confessions. He stands ready to "forgive our sins and cleanse us from all unrighteousness" (1 John 1:9).

We have described three types or methods of religious conversion, each including a wide range of personalities: (1) the experience of a child who emerged gradually into spiritual sensitivity and growth; (2) the rebirth of an intelligent God-seeker, stunned by a family crisis; and (3) the well-defined conversion experience of a person in later maturity. In every case salvation was viewed as God's gift and man's response. Each experience was distinctive and unique. Persons who choose the Christian way of life press forward "toward the goal for the prize of the upward call of God in Christ Jesus" (Phil. 3:14).

By contrast there are premature religious experiences that may be considered false "conversions." Stillborn, regressive, ungodly, and misguided converts usually require much more pastoral guidance and understanding than growing, healthy Christians. To be a disciple means more than saying yes to a formula or joining some church. One truly loves Christ who obeys his commandments and seeks to follow the will of God.

Ways to Witness

Opportunities for witnessing come to everyone. God makes his appeal through us as we respond to persons in spiritual distress and darkness (2 Cor. 5:20). The Christian's essential nature is like *salt* that flavors and preserves, like *light* that dispels dark guilt through the power of forgiveness (Matt. 5:13-16). Love lives patiently, yet courageously, among persons who need God's good news.

How does a believer witness to his faith in God in what Roger Shinn has called our "tangled world?" First, he must recognize that the world's hope does not lie in man's methods of renewal. The world's hope rests in the God and father of our Lord Jesus Christ. Again, as a student of God's Word, he must care profoundly about what God has done historically and is doing redemptively for his creation. As noted in chapter 3, caring is so personal that church members must be concerned about what is happening to people around them. It requires intelligence and courage to witness.

Since definition of any activity properly precedes action, we should agree upon what Christian witnessing is and is not. What I shall say is in the spirit of 1 Peter 3:15: "In your hearts reverence Christ as Lord. Always be prepared to make a defense to any one who calls you to account for the hope that is in you." We are to have a ready answer, yet listen to the sinner's questions, perceive his anxious longing, probe (with caution) his lost condition, then present Christ in the light of his particular needs. The gospel is like a surgeon's scalpel, not a broadax.

Witnessing is *not* just (1) talking about religion in general; (2) preaching (even Communists preach their faith); (3) visiting absentees or prospects; (4) attending church (which may be merely marking time); (5) asking someone "Are you a Christian?" (it's better to say, "Let me tell you about my Christian experience"); (6) tithing (which merely fulfils the Jewish law); (7) moralizing (citing sin statistics with an appeal to "quit your meanness"); (8) nor is it supporting the United Fund, Red Cross, and the United Nations. Such activities may become witnessing opportunities but are not essentially redemptive themselves.

In the *individual* sense, Christian witnessing is any means by which a Spirit-led person participates in or proclaims the good news that "God was in Christ reconciling the world to himself" (2 Cor. 5:19). It is done with a view of calling outsiders to salvation. There is a *corporate* witness, too, of an entire family, congregation, or community that relies upon the Holy Spirit to convince men of sin and turn them to Christ as Saviour. The key to witnessing is not in a single activity. Rather, it is a basic attitude, intention, and heartfelt desire that men might be saved. God can use anything we do to convict men of sin and turn them to righteousness, for the Holy Spirit is profoundly free (John 3:8).

You recall the discussion in chapter 4: visiting is witnessing, too. Practical suggestions were offered for those who wish to testify to their faith by calling in homes, apartments, and offices of prospective church members. Too, we witness with an intelligent faith, not sweet sentimentality nor pious catchwords. Few people are won to Christ with pet phrases and clever clichés. To have a "ready answer" suggests that we ought to inform ourselves of basic Bible beliefs, as well as of problems people face in secular society. The Holy Spirit has an affinity for a trained mind. It is unnecessary to out-argue a nonbeliever, but we should at least understand his line of argument.

We witness with an intelligent faith, by calling on the unsaved, and by the quality of our living. Christians are not weak, dependent, second-class citizens—unless they wish to be. The depth and serenity of one's spirit, the richness of his joy, the vitality of his daily output at work, the quality of his companions, the cleanness of his speech, the use of his talents and leisure, the loyalty to his family—what a person *is* communicates more eloquently than what he says or does alone. The psalmist wrote, "Let the redeemed of the Lord say so" (Psalm 107:2). Centuries later, Paul confessed his pride in the gospel: "It is the power of God for salvation to every one who has faith" (Rom. 1:16).

Too, we witness by corporate prayer and testimony in worship as well as by individual concern (see chapter 4). Finally, we witness by addressing the gospel to persons who are on the losing side in the struggle for existence. This includes all men—socially deprived, black and white, and the "up-and-outs" as well. Such persons are not merely drifting, unaffiliated, inactive, or unsaved. They are lost spiritually and condemned under the judgment of God. Yet he longs that all men might be saved (1 Tim. 2:4).

To *what* in lost sinners does evangelism address itself? Witnesses must know what people are moving *from* as well as what they are advancing *to*. Beneath the mask of people without God we find hollow, putty men and women who are pitifully weak and afraid. You may find: (1) moral chaos—lack of a "stackpole" around which life can be unified; (2) weakness of will—a lost man has little willpower to stop sinning. He tries but cannot save himself.

Usually there is (3) anxiety, for a person cut off from the land of the living experiences bondage to fear, dread of the unknown. Spiritual insecurity produces normal problems for some persons, neurotic symptoms in others. A state of anxious longing may be induced by feelings of guilt, conflicts within the self, and sense of separation from God. (4) Thus, loneliness—loss of fellowship with God, others, and one's best self—lies at the heart of a sin-burdened individual. He or she is literally cut off from the feast of life.

New Converts Grow

Jesus said to Nicodemus, "Unless one is born anew, he cannot see the kingdom of God" (John 3:3). Salvation transpires in the realm of grace rather than in any single method of witnessing. The "new birth" is a miracle of God's action that must be experienced to be understood. A convert has accepted himself as a sinner because he has experienced the forgiveness of God (Rom. 3:23, 6:23). Since he has been accepted by God, he affirms his own worth and responsibility by choosing God (Rom. 10:9-10).

Following this initial conversion experience, one is usually baptized and initiated (disciplined) into the life of a Christian congregation. Consider the experience of Tom McInnis, a seventy-three-year-old man in poor health, who lived on a ranch as a caretaker. He fed, watered, and guarded a herd of beef cattle for a wealthy landowner in a distant city. Everyone took for granted that Mr. McInnis would never become a Christian. He had been around for years. Everyone thought that he was too old, with the exception of a young pastor and his wife.

They took a personal interest in old Tom, built a bridge of friendship into his life, and sought him for the Saviour. Because he trusted their motives, Mr. McInnis attended their church services. Under conviction of God's Spirit, he responded to the invitation of the gospel and was baptized into the church's membership. Getting decisions like that is thrilling. But establishing new converts in the Christian life is not very dramatic. It takes months instead of minutes.

The zestful pastor becomes increasingly aware of varied needs of new church members like Tom McInnis. New converts need:

(1) Forgiveness—both human and divine—"at-one-ment;"

(2) Friendship with Christians—a sense of belonging;

(3) Fellowship in worship—a covenant relationship;

(4) Fortitude (steadfastness)—disciplined relationship with God;

(5) Faithful stewardship and opportunities for service. People grow toward spiritual security and maturity within a climate of acceptance, nurture, and mutual commitment.[3]

New converts grow but *not* automatically! They require individual attention. Adequate pastoral concern for new members is long overdue. This includes transplanted persons as well as new converts. People like Tom McInnis who join our churches deeply desire to make a go of their new way of life. Frequently, however, they drop out or drift away like Demas, who loved "this present world" and deserted Paul (2 Tim. 4:10). Often the failure has been not only with members who didn't stick, but with churches that failed to care.

What should your church do to prevent future failures and to encourage present members? Positively and preventively, churches should do more than merely offer new members a brief, formal acceptance into fellowship. In light of needs mentioned above, (1) a pastoral conference, following one's conversion experience, should precede his application for church membership. This is particularly urgent in the case of children, whose motives in seeking membership may not be clear. (2) One's reception into the church should be personal, reinforced with baptism and a certificate of membership.

(3) An orientation committee, composed of mature men and women, can meet with persons who present themselves for membership. It can provide information about the church's faith, history, life, and work, and, in turn, learn something about the new member. (4) A New Members' class, led by the pastor and selected associates, provides literature, group identification, participant conversation, and opens doors to friendship and service opportunities. (5) Christian education helps church members to move toward maturity as modern problems are faced in the light of biblical wisdom.

The establishment of a disciplined church membership procedure is the responsibility of the entire congregation, not the pastor or some group. Those who discipline persons toward maturity represent the congregation, not merely themselves. Elsewhere [4] I have discussed discipline in a negative or therapeutic sense. This concerns a distinct minority who "try out" life in the church, then give in to immorality. Every effort should be made to restore backsliders in a spirit of forgiving love (Gal. 6:1-2). One who continues to live a secular life should be recognized as no longer active in Christian fellowship. Properly, he does not have to be excluded from membership since he has already isolated himself from God's people. In time, such persons *may* be won back to the faith.

Bear One Another's Burdens

In the Galatians passage above, Christians are admonished to "bear one another's burdens, and so fulfil the law of Christ." Such a ministry of encouragement has both personal and group dimensions. In the chapters that follow we shall make explicit how Christian friends share life's private dramas and tragic crises. Here, we may observe that most of us stand in need of encouragement at least occasionally.

Think of some actual opportunities available to you for helping people of all ages, such as a child starting to school who soon shall leave home for the first time, a youngster who calls from camp reporting that he is homesick, a disobedient child that you must punish at home, your daughter's first big date, a youngster who has gotten his first speeding ticket, a son's failure to make a cherished team or a drop in grades at school, someone in a serious courtship who has been jilted, a student whose college career has been interrupted by military service, or a neighbor who has lost a loved one in death. Such persons need help of the right kind.

All about you people are making decisions, adjusting to hardship and change, facing experiences of hospitalization, coping with disappointing children (or parents), divorcing mates, declaring financial bankruptcy, and facing moral failures in their own lives. Where do such people gain the courage to live? What keeps them from serious crimes, while others commit illegal acts? What saves them from suicide? Do they not need the strengthening presence of God?

We do not know how great is the power of friendship and of forgiveness to renew a person's courage for life. Of course, it would be possible to spread oneself so thin in meeting such needs that one would not come to grips with real issues. As you live out your Christian existence, God can use your influence to keep people well, on course, and committed to him. A *friend*, someone said, is "one who comes in when the whole world has gone out." Like the relationship of David and Jonathan, a true friend "strengthens one's hand in God."

Some needs are greater than the resources of any single individual, family, or church. The pooled efforts of many people who care provide Christian hospitals, schools of higher education, and essential social ministries. Private groups occasionally form partnerships with wealthy foundations or public agencies in efforts to erase poverty, prevent mental illness, oppose juvenile delinquency, treat alcoholism, care for handicapped and retarded citizens, meet national emergencies like war and its aftermath, and recover from natural disasters like earthquakes and floods.

For example, in one city 485 members of the local Fire Fighter's Association purchased an eight-thousand-dollar mobile disaster canteen for the Salvation Army's use. The mobile unit is used when serving workers at a disaster scene. Trained personnel operate the unit, which is available for service anywhere in the state. Did the firemen who contributed toward the purchase of that vehicle of mercy perform a charitable service? Such deeds are based upon Christ's teachings, though they are not always performed out of Christian motives. This is also the case with social welfare programs sponsored by local, state, and national agencies.

The tithes and offerings of God's people are quickly translated into substantial deeds of love on home and foreign mission fields. A department of Christian social ministries has been established in our Home Mission Board that helps churches respond to the physical needs of people. Trained denominational employees work at inner-city centers; in the rehabilitation of juvenile delinquents, alcoholics, drug addicts, and ex-prisoners; in migrant ministries; literacy classes; disaster relief; and counseling and caring for girls or women who become pregnant out of wedlock. Recently, fifty thousand dollars was allocated for aid to hurricane-stricken churches in Louisiana. Is Christ concerned with persons in special need?

Some churches provide kindergartens for preschool children of working mothers, sewing circles, shop classes, and organized athletics for community youth. One church sponsors an integrated Vacation Church School each summer, attracting white and Negro pupils and teachers for Bible study and character-building activities.

Can people be attracted to Christ through such practical expressions of Christian love? Should a church limit its concerns to prospective members, or channel its energies in the direction of persons in need? There is much pressure on American church people to corrupt evangelism into a continuous success story. Rather than cooperating in healing and sustaining efforts, some churches compete with others in their communities. We face a grave danger of desiring instant success regardless of whether persons are truly converted.

Erik Routley has reminded us that the gap between mass evangelism and Christian conversion must be closed by the Holy Spirit, not by human techniques. Conversion, he writes, "is not enthusiasm. It is the process by which a man is received into the presence of God. . . ."[5] Churches should grow statistically *and* spiritually. Ministers are not content to serve a church "a mile wide and an inch deep," as one expressed it, because they experience endless frustration.

Pastors and laymen can determine to honor Christ, who gave his life a "ransom for many." Some persons whose lives they touch shall be healed, transformed. Others— sick, aged, grieved, handicapped—cannot be changed. What they need is a ministry of encouragement.

6

When Faith Encounters the Tragic

Theologians have been advising laymen to go "where the action is," but have offered limited wisdom about what to say or do when one lives outside the sanctuary.[1] Traditionally, laymen have worked *at* church performing tasks as varied as arranging flowers, purchasing Advent candles, counting money, teaching a class, cleaning church grounds, playing a piano, and keeping records. Much of the labor has been viewed as "leg work" for the pastor or "busy work" for the denomination.

One physician said, partly in jest, "My wife is the church worker in our family." He was so busy *being* the church to patients that he did not attend all church activities regularly. How does one get the substance of faith out of the church and into the secular affairs of daily life? In this chapter we shall explore ways that faith functions for the world's sake rather than for religion's sake alone.

Actually, little of a layman's working time is spent with religious problems per se. For example, the carpenter constructs houses, and the engineer designs gadgets. A teacher probes for new wisdom to share with students. The soldier in wartime tries to kill the enemy and, at the same time, to stay alive himself. A modern wife cares for endless chores, rears small children, and may work outside the home as well. A salesman advertises his products. The surgeon performs operations, and nurses provide postoperative care for patients. Activities like these appear mundane, secular. Yet a person's vocation is associated closely with his sense of identity and destiny—deeply spiritual matters. Furthermore, caring opportunities are wrapped within the relationships that any day brings.

Crises Are Common to Man

The private drama of one man's crisis provides a service opportunity for someone who cares. Again, some predicament or disaster may evoke a crisis of national proportions and require the intervention of a network of professional caregivers.

Biblical man was no stranger to tragedy and crises. The apostle James described the uncertainness of life, so easily cut down by disease, criminal assault, or some tragic accident. "You do not know about tomorrow. What is your life?" Phillips translates his answer: Life is like a "puff of smoke visible for a little while and then dissolving into thin air" (James 4:14*). Learning that life on this planet is temporary is a sobering lesson.

Some problems in human experience provoke emotional responses characterized by anxiety, disorganized thinking, and physical symptoms like fatigue, nausea, and sleeplessness. Or some predicament or decision forces some per-

---

* From The New Testament in Modern English, © J. B. Phillips, 1958. Used with permission of The Macmillan Company.

sons into a kind of immobilized state during which they show signs of strain, stereotyped thinking, even shock. How one handles such critical occasions is determined by his cultural heritage, personality strength, physical health, and religious faith.

One day during World War II, I walked on a bridge over the Thames River and saw London through the eyes of a stranger. No shapes on the horizon were familiar: St. Paul's, Trafalgar Square, Parliament, Hyde Park, Westminster Abbey. With the sensitivity of an outsider I absorbed details taken for granted by local citizens—domes, towers, lions, statues, ships, and parks. In previous years I had heard the strokes of Big Ben punctuate the day's passing hours via radio. That day the great clock's bell seemed strangely muffled in wartime. The city was like a giant picture puzzle with some of the bits out of place. Amid the millions of people, I felt uncomfortably alone; for the harvest of war pierced my heart.

That was a crisis experience imposed by painful separation from my family, isolation as a foreigner, the tragic sight of a besieged city, and the perilous environment of war. The whole world had been plunged into conflict. That day its burden and hurt became mine in a drama acted out within my own soul. Small wonder that I turned that evening to an American officer's club for companionship and support.

Events like the one above strip life of external wrappings and reveal the spirit of life itself. We call these experiences *crises*. The word "crisis," from the Greek *krisis* or *krinein,* "to separate," implies a turning point or decisive moment in experience. Medically, a crisis is that change in a disease which indicates whether the result is to be recovery or death. Life thrusts common (sometimes happy) crises upon us: graduation from school, marriage, a new job, the birth of a child, religious conversion, a promotion, winning some contest or award.

On the other hand, there are uncommon, often grievous, occasions that plunge a person, family, or entire community into distress. Violent acts of crime, fatal accidents, airplane crashes, mutilations and miseries of war, dreadful diseases, civil strife, or a loved one's death color experience a misty gray. Indeed, life is made up as much of what we must endure as of what we can enjoy. It is a bittersweet affair.

The private drama or crisis of which I speak is not the problem or provoking situation itself. Rather, it is the person's response to a situation, lasting from a few days to several months, and his eventual resolution of the matter.[2] Here are some problems which generally provoke crises: (1) Loss of basic needs or source of satisfaction— prompted by illness, death of a loved one, or dismissal from a job; (2) a threat (real or fancied) or risk of loss, such as a son's participation in battle, fear of theft, or forced retirement; (3) a challenge in which one is unable to cope with change, such as a job transfer, or to meet some obligation like a debt or deadline.

People cope with crises in varied ways—healthy and unhealthy. Here are some unhealthy ways.

1. One may deny the loss or threat by pretending it isn't there.

2. He may withdraw from normal relationships into a world of his own. Occasionally, devoted Christians are plunged into such a depressive state that they may resort to alcohol consumption, drugs, or the haunting fear that they are losing control. Such a person keeps asking himself, "Am I normal? Am I losing my mind?" They fear that they are "going crazy." Some persons feel so trapped that suicide seems to be the only way out.

3. He may develop bodily symptoms of illness requiring medical attention. This is the only way some people get sympathy or attention. Demands are relaxed while they are down; some families give strong support during a member's hospitalization. This person needs more than sympathy or impatience. He or she needs a protected environment, encouragement, support for sagging self-confidence, and opportunities to perform simple tasks to restore self-esteem. Thus, intervention—wise aid—by others is important at such times. The crisis blots out familiar landmarks. The individual may recover from struggle or shock but his resistance is down to outside influences which may weaken him.

While crisis experiences are common to everyone, we do not snap out of them easily or instantly. Much emotional and mental work is involved, and outside help may be needed. This means that people who care must remain alert to such circumstances and provide spiritual supports when needs are obvious. When ministering to another's need, his hurt can neither be fully explained nor explained away. It will help, however, to minister from the vantage point of Christian faith.

Faith and Suffering

For the Christian, fortunately, life's darkest patterns are silhouetted against the skyline of God's redemptive love. For too long pastors and others have proposed a limited solution to the tortured "Why?" of pained church members. "It is God's will," they reason emptily, which turns some trusting sufferers against God. A nursery worker in a church once dropped an infant given to her charge, and the injuries were fatal. The pastor, at an impasse in his own thinking, reasoned at the memorial service for the dead child: "God wanted another baby." If someone comes to you with what he calls "the simple gospel," offering neat rules and reasons for everything, distrust him. Human sorrow and divine response are never simple.

A clue to God's concern for man may be found in the cross. It was not for the comfort but the character of men that Christ went to the cross. If the pioneer of our salvation was made "perfect through suffering" (Heb. 2:10), God must have many lessons in store for us through pain. When it is accepted and rightly interpreted, suffering becomes a school of faith.[3] To miss its value as spiritual discipline, however, could permanently embitter an individual.

Crisis experiences hold both possibility and danger. Some persons mature through crucial situations, which C. S. Lewis, in *The Problem of Pain*, called "God's megaphone to rouse a deaf world." Do you recall King Hezekiah's illness, which he expected to be fatal? After his miraculous recovery the king recognized God's hand upon his life: "Lo, it was for my welfare that I had great bitterness" (Isa. 38:17). When one is unable to master a situation during the decisive stage of its occurrence, he shrinks or falls back in unbelief. Life's next problem then becomes more difficult to manage.

The Scriptures assure us that God does not remain aloof, unimpressed with human weakness and temptations. Here is a warning against idolatry, for example, that also contains assurance. "No temptation has overtaken you that is not common to man. God is faithful, and he will not let you be tempted beyond your strength, but with the temptation will also provide the way of escape, that you may be able to endure it" (1 Cor. 10:13). With this pledge of faithfulness to his covenant people goes God's promise to carry them through crises. "Cast your burden on the Lord, and he will sustain you" (Psalm 55:22, cf. Psalm 23). The pain which God is allowed to guide leads to his praise and our peace.

Perhaps you have asked along with Leslie Weatherhead and countless other believers across the ages, *Why Do Men Suffer?* There are endless lessons in pain that can be learned in perhaps no other school. We recognize that (1) *God permits suffering* for our good and his glory. Ultimately, we are dependent upon his providence and are assured that life has purpose. Theologian Roger Hazelton has said that "the tragic, if and when it comes, can be accepted at the hands of God." [4] Still, we do not understand why God permits one man to escape serious misfortune and requires another to have seemingly more than his share.

Again, (2) *God teaches his children through suffering*. In the Bible the chastening of God is viewed as fatherly discipline designed to bring people close to him (cf. Job 5:17; Prov. 3:11; Heb. 12:6-11). Chastisement is not really the same as punishment, yet some people feel sinned against by the Creator or life itself. Man was built for growth through his experiences, but we may see regression and resentment in some lives. Hurts come to everyone; how we handle the hurts is what counts. A hospitalized patient remarked: "God seems nearer to me than ever in my whole life." This is as it should be. Both Old and New Testament writers (cf. Lam. 3:32-33,40 and Rev. 3:19) were convinced that divine love lay beyond their pain, and urged their people to recognize this and return in repentance to God.

I should add that (3) *God transforms life through his own suffering in our stead.* The Christian faith finds its strength for facing the tragic in the cross. That "by his stripes we are healed" remains God's own mystery (Isa. 53:5; 1 Peter 2:24). That God should have embraced man's sins, sicknesses, and sorrows in the person of Jesus Christ is a note of triumph beyond tragedy. His incarnation, crucifixion, and resurrection reinforce us to meet any visitation of evil and suffering. He used tragedy to overcome tragedy and demonstrated voluntary, redemptive suffering for men. The resolution of evil (see Romans 8) lies in what God has been and is to us, despite our sin. He suffers with man, and for man, and aids him as he suffers.

Furthermore, crises prompt service on the part of family, friends, fellow church members, as well as professional "caretakers." In the biblical sense, the strong are aroused by suffering to stop suffering, as well as to "bear the burdens of the weak." We have no way of knowing how many persons the church keeps well! The church intervenes in crises when it knows such private dramas exist. Also, some troubles are detected early, in the initial stage, and treated preventively before they emerge full blown. Some situations, observed in religious education groups or in personal visits, may be faced squarely before they explode into crises.

Things to Avoid

Some persons possess a genius for friendship. They know when to call, to encourage, to speak, and to remain silent. They seem to show up when you need them most. Other individuals become a nuisance without really trying, annoying you with trite words or useless gifts. What is the difference? Is there a fault in your judgment so that you distrust some persons and put too implicit trust in others? No. Some individuals are endowed with intuitive wisdom, sensitive hearts, and compassionate hands. Would you like to become a better visitor, a more effective helper when crises come? Then—

1. *Don't go around looking for trouble.* It will find you. People confronted with decisions, like whether or not to accept a transfer; with sickness, like a wife's injury in an automobile accident; and with embarrassment, like that following a child's elopement, do not need nosiness. Curious onlookers at the scene of an accident generally get in the way rather than under the load. You can make your-

self or services available through a telephone call or visit, but don't insist on helping against someone's will.

2. *Don't pry into the details of other people's problems.* Some morbid individuals keep a few tears in store if only they can hear of a neighbor's tragedy. They gather gawkily to stare at the victim rather than to support him. Like Job's comforters, they collect details of the problem for gossip's sake rather than the victim's welfare.

If you have ever been offended by a curious inquisitor, then you know that certain secrets and hurts should not be shared. There is always a risk that someone, with defenses down in a crisis, will tell secrets but later resent anyone who knows the truth. If some sufferer trusts you with the headlines of his or her hurt, don't insist on reading the fine print, too.

3. *Don't preach.* When people ask "Why?" following a sad experience, they usually are expressing negative emotions, *not* seeking information. Neighbors beaten down by life's problems need not exhortation nor judgment but the healing silence of God. "I appreciate your prayer," responded a hospitalized accident victim, "because you didn't shout. . . ." "No," I replied, "God has good ears. He knows what we need."

4. *Don't belittle a troubled person.* Persons who need help usually give clear signals that they are in trouble. A young wife who fears pregnancy will hint this to her physician or to a fellow employee where she works. A teen-age lad, whose parents in California had separated, suddenly showed up in Texas at a friend's house. "May I live here and go to school with you next year?" he im-

plored a buddy. In appraising the situation the boy's older sister explained that he had been trapped. "There just wasn't enough love in our family to go around," she observed. When troubles impede life's progress, persons attempt to remove the obstruction. They need understanding and assistance, not ridicule. Don't reject or belittle such persons. Give or get the help they need.

5. *Don't press the object of your aid into your mold.* I once heard of an executive who employed a public relations man in another state. Soon after the new employee showed up at work, his powerful, wealthy boss enforced certain company rules. One rule insisted that all employees participate in the John Birch society. There were many others. Without hesitation, the public relations man quit the job in order to retain his freedom and self-respect as a person.

Helpers occasionally seek power over the weak objects of their care. Parents dominate sons or daughters via long distance, after they are grown and gone from home. Mercy is shown a debtor *if* certain provisions in the contract are carefully kept. Interestingly, Jesus Christ warned his disciples not to "lord" it over other people, such as pagans. The Scriptures teach us to "encourage the fainthearted, help the weak, be patient with them all" (1 Thess. 5:14). But nowhere are we taught to remake persons in our own image. We are to be mutual followers of Christ and workers together with God (2 Cor. 6:1). The primary commitment of the helped and helpers alike should be to God, to basic values, and to Christian goals.

The unconscious urge for power presses pastors and

laymen to gain control of people's lives. Remind yourself before any pastoral call that the object of your concern remains a person, *not* your pawn. Don't remind him of aid given in the past or of what he owes you for all of your assistance to him. Gratitude and responsible behavior on his part must appear voluntarily. Do what you can, pray, and trust God to guide and provide for added needs.

Courage to Care

We can expect a lack of certainty about Christian obligations in a day of change. Some of the supports for religious attitudes and practices that we relied on previously were thought to be essentials of our Christian faith. Now we realize that they were simply cultural expressions of this faith, and the culture is changing. Can we be *both* faithful to the essentials of the Christian message *and* flexible in its communication in the modern world? What attitudes will assist us in courageous caring?

Let's be realistic.—We have said that Christ's ministry continues in all the world, for all time, through all of his disciples. The mission of the Master's first followers is described in the tenth chapter of Matthew. Their assignment was (1) to preach that "the kingdom of heaven is at hand;" (2) to heal the sick, cleanse lepers, cast out demons, and raise the dead; (3) to travel light, staying in homes that offered hospitality; and (4) to watch out for trouble. Jesus warned them that they would run into hatred and persecution among the "lost sheep of the house of Israel."

Jesus' parting warning buried itself in their minds: "Behold, I send you out as sheep in the midst of wolves; so be wise as serpents and innocent as doves" (Matt. 10:16). Our Lord taught as much by paradox as in parable. A paradox, rather than a clear statement of fact, is a riddle—an apparent contradiction. We see the clash of opposites merge toward a sharply focused point of truth. What did the Teacher from Nazareth mean by this seeming contradiction?

Perhaps his hidden meaning will become clear in a phrase from a eulogy voiced by a pastor at the memorial service for an honored deacon. "This man was both tenderhearted and tough-minded," said the minister. "He felt deeply for people who needed the Saviour, yet he was careful where he invested his time, wealth, and energy." That Christian layman could be moved to tears by stories of spiritual need. Yet, as he served on committees of church agencies, he was cautious with his own and his denomination's resources. Facts, not sentimentality, formed the basis for his decisions.

How can a sensitive Christian be both tenderhearted (a dove) and tough-minded (a serpent) at the same time? Take the following example. A lawyer, reared in the chivalrous South, was transferred to New York by the insurance company he represented. Since his family preferred living in a Long Island residential community, the attorney commuted one hundred miles round trip each day.

During one afternoon rush at the commuter gates of Pennsylvania Station, he saw an elderly woman spill the contents of a shopping bag. People rushed around them as he stopped to help her recover the items scattered on the floor. "What do you think you're doing?" came her retort. "I can get them myself!" Her rude resistance to his attentiveness stunned the lawyer. Some time later he said to a friend, "I'll know next time not to try to help these Yankees." The idealist was becoming a realist!

"Did he lose his idealism in one nasty incident?" you may wonder. No, but his concern for other persons took on a new quality—a caution geared to the New Yorker's way of life. "Helpers" in the metropolis are often wolves in sheep's clothing—hoodlums who later attack the victim of their false kindness, or swindlers who hoodwink a naïve newcomer. The independence of city dwellers and their reserve or dislike for strangers may be observed in any great city of the world. Yet, contrary to some opinions, they are not unfriendly.

Here is the reason that Jesus put great value on wisdom and purity of heart. One who appears in the costume of a helper—whether a parent, employer, teacher, a nation's chief executive, or an ordinary citizen—may be rebuffed by the very people he would aid. An idealistic missionary to the inner city may be crushed by the indifference of the multitudes there. Laws of the city jungle reverse the spirit of the Golden Rule: "Do it to others before they can get to you." The pages of Christian history are littered with stories of martyrs, like Bill Wallace of China, who went to help and died in enemies' hands. Therefore, people who care must be realistic.

Some people will "use" you.—A Christian's generosity may be consumed ungratefully by a dependent person, or perverted for selfish purposes by someone with ulterior motives. A layman who works in the field of Christian communications received an inquiry about a broadcast from a native of Southeast Asia. Taking the inquirer at face value, he began a correspondence with the man that lasted ten years. Mr. Woo prevailed upon him to assist with the transportation and education of several children in the United States. Finally, he himself came to this country, bringing his youngest daughter. He sensed the value of education and, at age fifty-three, enrolled as a student in a state university.

"What do you hear from Mr. Woo?" I inquired recently. "Nothing," replied my friend. "We corresponded regularly for ten years until he came to this country. Now I never hear from him. Perhaps," he added wistfully, "Mr. Woo got what he wanted and has no further use for my friendship." Those of us who attempt Christian service may be abused by some objects of our care. A critic might call the above layman a do-gooder, and say of Mr. Woo's manipulation, "I told you so." This is a risk we take. Courage must be mixed with wisdom and tempered by caution.

Keep your love alive.—Our Lord advocated innocence (purity of heart) for his servants, but not ignorance. And he applauded neither deception nor cunning but authentic concern, redemptive involvement in the hurt of man. Persons who grapple in hand-to-hand combat with the evil forces of life must have confidence in divine resources. When we do God's work today, his Spirit touches our own and transforms our efforts into human good.

How can the simplicity and tenderness of the dove be

nurtured, even kept alive, in the brittle climate of scientific precision, social welfare caring, and suspicious distrust? Schoolchildren are warned to avoid "strangers" who might harm them on the way to school. Gangs of young people arm themselves with all sorts of weapons and plan strategies of escape or counterattack in the event they are challenged by an enemy. Housewives forbid bell-ringing salesmen to enter their defenseless apartments or homes because some innocents have become victims of vicious assaults. Automobile drivers are warned not to pick up hitchhikers, for some have aided robbers and murderers unawares.

Someone wrote, "Love is what you do." How do you square that with the fact that Protestants generally are nonrevolutionary people who talk rather than revolutionary people who act? A young minister and his wife were appointed to missionary service in Japan. When he arrived in Tokyo, the world's largest city, he was shocked with the treatment of women in the Far East. "Stay tender as long as you can," advised an associate. "Soon you will see them abused and it won't matter anymore." People grow scales over their eyes so that they no longer see running sores in their communities. It is easy to be victimized by the status quo, to keep what one has for himself alone, to become numb to life's private dramas.

Persons in need are all around you. You can discover easily whether or not other persons or agencies are involved in the same crisis. Determine the needs which you can meet best, and share responsibility for others with fellow church members and professional caretakers.

7

Sharing Life's Private Dramas

A modern Christian finds it difficult to believe in the *living* God in a world of thermonuclear politics, space exploration, social planning, and returning nationalism. He tends to read the day's headlines without mustering faith to meet or view the situation. How easy it is to restrict God to the period during which the Bible was written, and religion to church attendance on Sunday. Yet God becomes relevant for us precisely when we see him "between the lines" of individual decisions and group struggles today. That has been this book's concern.

Foregoing chapters have challenged us to detect God's action in current crises and social dilemmas. We have identified the work that a church should do. In the second chapter we sought an appropriate response to the question: What does it mean to be God's people today? The necessity of a united witness to Christ, cooperative social action, and organized activities for helping people have been acknowledged. Yet there is no substitute for personal concern.

We shifted in chapter 4 to caring skills: counseling, visitation, prayer, correspondence, and referral to specialists. In subsequent chapters we explored caring opportunities during religious conversion, character development, and personal crises.

We would now like to offer specific suggestions for coping with three typical crises: marriage conflict, hospitalized illness, death and bereavement.

Marriage Conflict

From the earliest recorded experiences of man misunderstandings have arisen between husbands and wives, parents and children. Situations occur in the course of life that appear intolerable. Those who believe in do-it-yourself therapy tell overburdened people that, with a little positive thought, these perils can be met. But marital conflict will not go away or clear up easily.

A licensed vocational nurse employed at a Protestant hospital became acquainted with a nursing supervisor and her husband, Mr. and Mrs. Cecil Slaton. Over a period of months the LVN, whom we shall call Mrs. Morris, discovered that she could trust the Slatons. One afternoon they exchanged greetings in the hospital cafeteria.

They noted that she was taking medication with a cold drink, and she said that a psychiatrist had prescribed tranquilizers for her nerves. After a brief exchange, Mrs. Morris confided to them her marital problems.

Apparently, Mrs. Morris was suffering enough to bear her heart to the Slatons. It would appear that she sought support and spiritual encouragement rather than profound insight into her family problems.

She did not know where to turn and received only

limited help from the Slatons. But at least she was able to see much of the marital picture, with all of its sick dimensions, in perspective through conversation. And Mrs. Morris agreed to make an appointment with a Christian marriage counselor before she left.

What may appear to be the number one conflict in a marriage is often only one expression of more *basic problems* rooted in the personality structure of each spouse. Such problems often defy identity, yet they cluster in three broad areas. Personal, cultural, and situational factors contribute to marriage conflict.

Personal factors include inadequate motives for marriage, degree of maturity, commitment, religious differences, money, sex, work, alcohol, mental and physical health.

Cultural factors underlying marriage conflict include: (1) a family's values (influenced more often by social class structure rather than by religious convictions); (2) mobility, which breeds a feeling of rootlessness, not belonging, and consequent irresponsibility; (3) differences in educational, vocational, and recreational interests; (4) early dating privileges and earlier marriages, with consequent boredom and opportunities for infidelity; and (5) the ease of getting a divorce in most states, accompanied by a lost sense of responsibility for one's spouse and children.

In the Morris case above, for example, she was seventeen when they married; and she married against the advice of her family and his brothers, who called him "irresponsible." Willie was a lay-preacher who could sound holy on Sunday, but who had a character disorder so severe that he tried to seduce his own daughter, as he did other women, many times. In a case like this, Mrs. Morris probably stayed with her mate for the children's sake and for status' sake, rather than for personal satisfactions gained in the relationship.

Situational factors, like separation because of work schedules or war, family complications, and psychic injuries brought about or complicated by infidelity also affect marriage adjustment. Enough things are involved to make a self-help therapy program appear useless, though personal initiative and responsibility are essential to family change and harmony. Some situations and people do not change, as in Willie Morris' case. Their mates and children either muster enough strength to survive, leave home, or become ill even to the point of suicide.

Marriages are "made in heaven," someone said, but they are also made or broken on earth in the small talk and deeds of daily living. When a family needs help in the process of conflict, one or both mates should talk with their pastor or trusted friend like a physician. Failures in adjustment in the early years can be worked out privately *if the marriage has been founded on a covenant of integrity.* When isolation symptoms appear—feeling sorry for oneself, blaming the other partner, or projecting hostility onto a child or mate—the couple should seek assistance.

Actual separation is an open admission of failure. A legal separation for a few weeks or months may be therapeutic, however, providing time for the partners to work through hurt feelings or conflicts. Some homes can be saved if conflict can be neutralized and negative feelings are reversed. The children tend to suffer most.

Once a divorce has been obtained, persons involved experience a grief reaction more difficult to bear than death itself. A partner may act relieved that the case is settled, but his or her feelings about the conflict are far from settled. Regaining one's balance may require months, not days.

People like yourself, who try to understand and help divorcees, realize that problems which have taken a lifetime to develop are not solved in one interview. That is hoping for too much. If divorce comes, encourage the admission of failure and need for change and growth prior to remarriage. Some mates will not marry a second time. Others will mature through mistakes, admit the sinfulness of the situation, seek forgiveness—human and divine—and start life over in a new marital relationship.

Hospitalized Illness

Whether you enter a hospital as a patient or as a visitor, you will increase your effectiveness by considering certain facts. *One*, while accidents and illnesses are common occurrences from the hospital's perspective, they are not customary for your neighbors. Hospitalized illnesses and surgical procedures disrupt life's serenity and threaten the security of persons and their families. Causes of illness or injury vary: industrial accident, gunshot wound, accidental burn or fall, infection of a vital organ, and invasion by disease. "If it's *my* toe that's being cut on," someone quipped, "then it's *major* surgery." For most folks, going to the hospital provokes a crisis. Life's customary anxieties are intensified.

The nature of one's condition, in the *second* place, determines his attitudes toward hospitalization and needs as a patient. An executive's annual checkup in the medical center is a preventive measure, involving temporary dislocation from work, but it is not a threatening trip. An aged father being placed permanently in a convalescent home—against his will—provokes a unique set of responses in him and his children. Removal of a child's tonsils has become a simple procedure, requiring overnight hospitalization. Open-heart surgery on the family breadwinner, on the other hand, is another matter.

You do not have to know the exact nature or details of a patient's condition in order to visit effectively. Simply remember, when calling, that *acute* illnesses usually involve short term hospitalization, and the *chronic* conditions may persist even when a patient returns home.

Three, the patient's capacity for coping with the upset, accident, or surgical procedure will determine the degree of crisis he or she experiences. Some people imagine the worst; they fear cancer or, in case of anxiety, fear they are going crazy. Your own relationships with the patient and family will determine how effective and useful you can be during the illness.

As you visit a patient or family member, you can determine his maturity and spiritual resources for facing the situation. You will see patients deny death, hoping that God or the doctor will work a miracle. Others will be hostile, asking: "Why did God permit this to happen?" To such a soul-searching question you might reply, "Tell me what you think." Dependency needs will be evidenced.

"We just don't know how to appreciate good health," someone might say. Another will confess, "If it weren't for God and my good neighbors, I don't know what I'd do."

Guilt can be detected in some families. "God let Charlie fall because . . . ," they rationalize, trying to connect a single sin with a specific accident. This is impossible, because the innocent suffer along with the guilty. All sin brings suffering, but all suffering is not the result of sin. You or I may suffer, not because of our sin but because of someone else's fault—as in an automobile accident, for example. It is encouraging to work with families facing illness who say: "Joe is sick. With God's help he can be well."

When you enter the halls of a modern hospital remember that the combined efforts of the entire medical and nursing staffs are aimed at restoring health, prolonging life. You represent God and a specific church—redemptive group—in the midst of a healing environment. Thus you will wish to be a wholesome guest in a person's private or semiprivate room, as well as an effective spiritual instrument during the visit.

Visit the sick not as a pious habit or good deed for the day but with the intent of supporting the patient or family in the lonely hospital setting. (*Support* is not to be confused with reciting jokes, sharing gossip, or divulging morbid details of a mutual friend's dying condition.)

All of us have visited enough to recognize that *we are not indispensable to the patient's recovery*. In protecting the patient's welfare, hospital visitors will be guided by the following principles.

1. Respect the hospital's policy about time for visitation. Schedules are enforced in obstetrics and nursery departments to protect the welfare of women after labor and childbirth, and to reduce infection among infants.

2. Secure information about patients prior to entering a room. Correct room assignments are provided through an information service. If a door is closed, knock before entering. A nurse or aide may assist you with information about the person or in gaining admission to the room.

3. Heed signs on the door, such as Isolation, X-ray, No Visitors, and the call light. They are placed at the room's entrance to protect the patient, to prolong his life, and to inform personnel if the patient has been taken to another department.

4. Introduce yourself as you are received into the sickroom. Some patients under the influence of drugs or sedatives may be woozy or asleep. Aged patients or accident victims may not recall your name or even recognize you. Since this is his or her private room and the host is sick, be at your best.

5. Remember that patients are unduly sensitive because of pain, uncertainty, infection, and so on. Do not say anything knowingly that will linger in the patient's mind and worry him after your departure. If the patient appears asleep or unconscious or does not respond, his hearing faculties may still be at work. It is best to visit with family members outside the room in cases of critical illness.

6. Just because you are up and the patient is down, don't assume a patronizing air toward the sick person. You may be next! Be genuine in your interest and concern.

Seek to represent God faithfully in that particular patient's case. For example, avoid clichés or stock comments.

7. Stand or sit in the patient's line of vision. Be friendly to others in the room but, where possible, concentrate upon a face-to-face ministry with the patient. Avoid leaning on the bed or jarring equipment like an infusion flask or an oxygen tent.

8. The frequency and length of your hospital visits will be determined by varied factors: the distance of your residence from the hospital, relationship to the patient, his or her capacity to receive company, and so on. No one can tell you how long a visit should be. Its duration will vary according to the patient's condition and responsiveness, interruptions, and presence of other visitors.

You may desire to leave a card or gift as a token of your affection for the patient. When our son was a second grader, years ago, his teacher visited him during a period of hospitalization. She brought picture greetings from his fellow pupils in elementary school, and an ivy plant in a dog-shaped container. He was too weak from fever and infection to say much at the time, but he cherished those tokens of friendship and love in days of recovery.

Normally, the antennae of a person's soul are extremely sensitive to signals from God and his servants during illness. You will not have to carry God into a sickroom. He is already present in the midst of the treatment situation. If you wish to read the Scriptures or voice a prayer, don't use such resources as a means to escape from the room. These are not contrivances for avoiding uncomfortable relationships. They are "at home" in any relationship which recognizes God in the midst (Matt. 18:20) and seeks to honor his name. In a sense, the entire visit should be conducted in the spirit of prayer, recalling that "from the most high comes healing."

Death and Bereavement

I called upon a cancer patient whom the physicians had pronounced terminally ill. She talked of getting stronger and returning to her Junior High school teaching activities. "What if it should go the other way, Mary Ann?" I inquired, deliberately giving that lovely woman an opportunity to talk about her death—if she desired. "Oh, it won't," she denied, refusing to speak of life's end. The desire to avoid references to death led her to talk about little things that gave meaning to each day.

Biblical man viewed biological death as a dreadful certainty resulting from sin, and looked uncertainly to life beyond death. Second Samuel 14:14 records a dialogue between a king and a woman of Tekoa: "We must all die; we are like water spilt on the ground, which cannot be gathered up again." The ancient preacher mused, "The living know that they will die" (Eccl. 9:5); and the psalmist anticipated, "The years of our life are threescore and ten" (Psalm 90:10). Allusions to death are like mist upon the mountains in the Wisdom literature. Life is "like grass . . . a flower . . . the wind . . . like a river wasting away."

Resolute hope appears in New Testament writings where death is swallowed up in the victory of eternal life. This apostolic hope was based upon Christ's teachings and his acknowledged resurrection from the grave.

Man's attitudes toward death are determined largely by his socio-historical background and religious beliefs. In humanistic thought death is the end of all existence. Such materialistic conclusions are certified by dissolution of the body's cellular and chemical components at death. Victorian man's anxious longings for immortality appear in the works of Browning and Tennyson. Romantic poets like Byron and Shelley courted death. Modern Americans are in the process of making up their minds about the mystery of death.

When Abraham Lincoln lived, the average life expectancy was forty-five to fifty. Now, it is seventy to seventy-five in the United States, with promise of an almost indefinite life span. Americans seek immortality, are told to "think young." Still—the living know that they will die. Death is no stranger. Rather, as reported in a *Time* essay, it is our constant companion (Nov. 12, 1965, pp. 52-53). Death never takes a holiday.

Death is often in the thoughts of church members, yet seldom in their conversations. The subject can be suppressed, yet it invades one's dreams as a phantom from a far-off planet. Whatever one says of death will be both right and wrong. It will *not* be the voice of experience. Much data is not merely unknown but unknowable.

We do not know, for example, when a person is supposed to die. Doctors attending a female patient in her late twenties told her parents that, according to her longevity curve and condition, she should be dead. But she defied every estimated deadline they set. Their explanation? "She is young and has a great will to live."

We do not know when a person gives up hope. For example, we are not sure how much of a suicide's self-system has been destroyed before physical death occurs. Psychologist James Hillman theorizes that, in philosophic thought, *"all death is suicide,* and the choice of method is only more or less evident, whether car-crash, heart-attack, or those acts usually called suicide." [1] You and I would observe, to the contrary, that many deaths are accidental, others result from disease, and that infants' deaths are not suicidal.

On the other hand, the suicidal person may not be aware that he or she is killing himself. A chaplain of a state psychiatric hospital told some friends of having been ticketed three times recently for excessive speeding. "I may want to leave that place more than I'll admit," he said jestingly.

Some persons drive themselves mercilessly without honestly recognizing that death is their goal. Others are impatient with this life. They demand a fuller life, freedom from this world, by choosing how and when they shall die. Suicide becomes a way of escape for twenty thousand or more Americans each year. In addition to the successful suicides, there are several times that number of attempted suicides. Some cities, like Los Angeles, have established Suicide Prevention Centers in an attempt to cope with this problem.

The moment a child is born he is old enough to die—an Rh factor gone awry, suffocation or strangulation, congenital malformation, or birth trauma. For some persons dying is drawn out over months of waiting—cancer, heart disease, stroke. Perhaps there is time to put one's house in order. Yet, in much of modern dying, there is no conscious moment of death. Rather, there may be prolonged coma or life is snuffed out instantly. This is true of mass bombings in war, victims of criminal attack, a flaming automobile wreck, the victims of an airliner's crash, or a ship's sinking into a watery grave.

Trying to cope with death raises perplexing questions. Scientists have confirmed the biblical assertion that we are always dying and being renewed (2 Cor. 4:16). While physicians soften our dreadful anticipation of dying by placing terminally ill persons in medical settings, out of sight; while frozen interment promises limited immortality; [2] while mourning has been modified by sedation and the grief process interpreted by psychiatrists,[3] man cannot forever repress his questions. One can take his mind off things just so long.

Ministers presiding at memorial services for man's final "rite of passage" know that they are skirting the edges of a great mystery. For the survivors, who shrink from the dark abyss, death in imagination is a reality. Anxieties about death must be faced by the church. No matter how we seek to outwit it with substitute forms of immortality (art, sex, influence) death will not be denied its harvest.

People who care cope with a multitude of responses from the dying and members of the family.

1. *Some persons deny death's reality.* They are in love with life. For example, a youth of twenty—recently married and a senior in college—was injured fatally in an automobile accident. What were Richard's last words be-

fore lapsing into a coma? "Don't cheat me, God," his family and intimate friends heard him pray, "I want to live." Soon his room was filled with stillness. Life faded like a vapor in the morning sun.

To escape death we find a scapegoat, like the funeral directors in Jessica Mitford's *The American Way of Death.* A current movie *The Loved One* turns death into a joke. And the plot of playwright Ionesco's *How to Get Rid of It* concerns a corpse that grows and grows until it floats away like a giant balloon.

2. *The living generally do not want to burden their family and friends.* Some men prepare elaborately through legal advice for estate settlement. Even the poor hope to be buried decently, yet quietly. If you listen to the whispered words between friends in a hospital waiting room, there is a desire to avoid suffering. "I hope that God takes me quickly," admits one. "I don't want to burden my family." The neighbor agrees, "Yes, I hope that I don't suffer like so-and-so."

3. *In a world of gigantic death we find many people hardened to the subject.* They bring to death what they bring to life—a materialistic outlook. This is true in war-torn lands. In America, the child who watches TV westerns, gangster and war films becomes toughened to death's tragic dimensions. He never sees anyone really die, nor an animal unless a pet is injured fatally by a car. Imagine his response to the news that grandfather is dead. "Who shot him?" he might ask in Matt Dillon fashion.

4. *Some people insist that the power of life and death remains in their hands.* This is true of any physician who

has practiced any form of mercy-killing, including withdrawal of life-extending drugs or equipment from terminally ill patients. The suicide, as we have said, may view his exit from earth as an act of courage—thoughtfulness for his family or mercy for himself. Violent men, whether criminals or temporarily insane, treat life indifferently. Before he died, ex-marine Charles Whitman killed fifteen persons—including his wife and mother—and wounded thirty-one more from his sniper's post at the University of Texas. *Life* magazine called that monstrous event the most savage one-man rampage in the history of American crime (Aug. 12, 1966, pp. 24-31).

5. Perhaps you have known *persons who faced death with courage mixed with dread and misgivings.* Such was the case of a Christian minister who knew that he was dying. "I know that the time is short, Dr. Kline," said the fifty-year-old minister whom we shall call George. "I do not want to prolong my life with humane drugs and modern gadgets."

The two agreed that the patient would remain at work and at home with his family as long as possible. One Friday, a friend stopped by his office. "How is it going, George?" he inquired. "I can't complain," replied the dying man, who refused to give in to pain and depressive feelings. Within a week he was gone. A humanistic observer might call that stoicism. To us it appears to have been courageous Christian realism.

This experience raises the question of whether or not to tell a person that death is near. Members of the health team do not agree on this ethical question. I believe that sick persons have a right to know the truth to the limit of their ability to bear it. I have talked with a score or more physicians about this matter. With few exceptions, they let each patient know the truth and assist him to live as fully as possible with the truth. Yet, doctors can be wrong. Cause and effect laws do not operate identically in all people. Resistance to illness differs with each patient. Thus, it is best to face critical illnesses with skilled medical attention and realistic Christian assurance.

There are grief experiences in life more oppressive than death: divorce, delinquency, infidelity, invalidism, or mental illness, for example. Comforters of those who mourn should understand that the process of grief works so that its developmental stages may be met with appropriate resources.[4] Normal expressions of grief—shock, protests, tears, stereotyped thinking, anxious dependence, and impulsive talking about the deceased—permit a healthy cleansing of emotions. The widow who sits tearlessly through a funeral service, unable to express her true feelings, may find herself deeply depressed in future weeks.

Grief's wound has been called "the illness that heals itself." Under appropriate conditions of support within a community of love the bereaved person is free to work through his or her loss. Bereavement properly becomes *grief work* when a person, rather than avoiding reality, (1) accepts his loss and the suffering that goes with it, (2) consolidates memories of the past with future plans, and (3) assumes responsibility for life's new demands. Thus, repressive words, including the misuse of the Scriptures, should be avoided. When a person's heart is broken he needs not explanations but friends who will stand by, plus the healing silence of God. When grief has its work, through the resources of the Christian funeral and after-care, life must go on.

Conclusion

The Christian faith faces numerous challenges today: organized evil and social injustice, lawlessness and inhumanity, indifference within and opposition without. Critics of the church argue that life's real issues should be met by social planners, economists, politicians, and militarists, not by ministers or laymen.

This book has dared us to admit that a Christian's role as a public citizen cannot be separated from his private life. The new and future minister or layman will not merely argue for the Ten Commandments and New Testament faith. People who care will act upon their convictions and involve themselves in human needs—private and public. Their goal is that the *helped* become *helpers*. In a climate of love they advance the kingdom of God.

Notes

Chapter 1

1. See G. Avery Lee's constructive discussion *What's Right with the Church?* (Nashville: Broadman Press, 1967).

2. "Are the Churches in Trouble?" *U. S. News and World Report* (April 18, 1966), pp. 54-60.

3. Claude Welch, *The Reality of the Church* (New York: Charles Scribner's Sons, 1958), p. 16.

4. Bonhoeffer, leader in the German resistance movement, was executed by the Nazis on April 9, 1945, at the age of thirty-nine.

5. Peter F. Drucker, *Landmarks of Tomorrow* (New York: Harper & Row [Colophon edition], 1965), p. xi.

6. Arthur Miller, *The Death of a Salesman* (New York: Viking Press, 1958).

7. See W. O. Carver's introduction to *What Is the Church?* ed. Duke K. McCall (Nashville: Broadman Press, 1958), p. 5; cf. also pp. 1-14.

Chapter 2

1. See Hendrik Kraemer, *A Theology of the Laity* (Philadelphia: Westminster Press, 1958), pp. 160-64.

2. *Help! I'm a Layman* (Waco, Texas: Word Books, 1966).

3. See Martin E. Marty, *The New Shape of American Religion* (New York: Harper & Row, 1958); also, his *Second*

Chance for American Protestants (New York: Harper & Row, 1963).

4. Altizer is coauthor with William Hamilton of *Radical Theology and the Death of God* (Indianapolis: Bobbs-Merrill Co., 1966).

5. See Dietrich Bonhoeffer, *Letters and Papers from Prison* (originally entitled *Prisoner for God*), ed. Eberhard Bethge, trans. R. H. Fuller (New York: Macmillan Co., 1962).

6. For example, see Peter L. Berger, *The Noise of Solemn Assemblies* (New York: Doubleday & Co., 1961); also his *The Precarious Vision* (New York: Doubleday & Co., 1961), which deals with the individual in society.

7. William Stringfellow, *A Private and Public Faith* (Grand Rapids, Mich.: Wm. B. Eerdmans Publishing Co., 1962), p. 75.

Chapter 3

1. Peter de Vries, *The Mackerel Plaza* (Boston: Little, Brown & Co., 1958), pp. 4, 7-8.

2. By this term I imply "pastoral care," not in the restrictive sense of a ministers-only function, but in the general sense of a *perspective* that gives depth and direction to all human relationships.

Chapter 4

1. The *Baptist Student* is published by The Sunday School Board, Nashville, Tennessee; cf. also *Motive,* Methodist student publication.

2. See Paul Tournier, *The Adventure of Living,* trans. Edwin Hudson (New York: Harper & Row, 1965).

3. Mrs. Warner E. Fusselle, a homemaker and pastor's wife in Gainesville, Georgia, "My Bible Class in Jail," *The Adult Teacher* (May, 1962), pp. 6-9.

4. If you wish to explore this subject, read Karl Barth, *Prayer,* trans. Sara F. Terrien (Philadelphia: Westminster Press, 1962),

or prayer classics by writers like Harry Emerson Fosdick, John S. Bonnell, Charles Allen, and George Buttrick.

Chapter 5

1. See Samuel Southard's helpful discussions in *Pastoral Evangelism* (Nashville: Broadman Press, 1962) and *Conversion and Christian Character* (Nashville: Broadman Press, 1965).

2. David E. Roberts, *Psychotherapy and a Christian View of Man* (New York: Charles Scribner's Sons, 1950), p. 132.

3. See, for example, Findley Edge's *A Quest for Vitality in Religion* (Nashville: Broadman Press, 1963); Lewis J. Sherrill, *Guilt and Redemption,* rev. ed. (Richmond, Va.: John Knox Press, 1957); D. Elton Trueblood, *The Company of the Committed* (New York: Harper & Row, 1961).

4. See *Pastoral Care in the Church* (New York: Harper & Row, 1964), pp. 26-28, 208-13. Cf. also James Leo Garrett, *Baptist Church Discipline* (Nashville: Broadman Press, 1962).

5. Erik Routley, *The Gift of Conversion* (Philadelphia: Muhlenberg [now Fortress] Press, 1958), pp. 136-37.

Chapter 6

1. An exception is the valuable work by William M. Pinson, *How to Deal with Controversial Issues* (Nashville: Broadman Press, 1966). Cf. Harvey Cox, *God's Revolution and Man's Responsibility* (Valley Forge, Pa.: Judson Press, 1965).

2. The writer is indebted to Edward Norman, M. D., professor of psychiatry, Tulane Medical School, for insights from an address given in Nashville, Tennessee, September 28, 1965, entitled "Crisis Intervention in Pastoral Counseling."

3. For this idea the writer is indebted to T. B. Maston, whose manuscript on suffering was unpublished at the time of this writing.

4. Roger Hazelton, *God's Way with Man* (Nashville: Abingdon Press, 1956), p. 155.

Chapter 7

1. James Hillman, *Suicide and the Soul* (New York: Harper & Row, 1964), p. 62.

2. Robert C. W. Ettinger, "The Frozen Christian," *The Christian Century* (October 27, 1965), pp. 1313-15; cf. also his *The Prospect of Immortality* (Garden City, N. Y.: Doubledav & Co., 1964).

3. Erich Lindemann, "Symptomatology and Management of Acute Grief," *American Journal of Psychiatry*, 101 (1944), 141-48.

4. See author's discussion in *Pastoral Care in the Church* (New York: Harper & Row, 1964), pp. 249-55.